W9-AVK-339

Will.i.am

Will.i.am

The Unauthorized Biography

DANNY WHITE

MICHAEL O'MARA BOOKS

First published in Great Britain in 2012 by
Michael O'Mara Books Limited
9 Lion Yard
Tremadoc Road
London SW4 7NQ

A CIP catalogue record for this book is available from the British Library.

Papers used by Michael O'Mara Books Limited are natural, recyclable products made from wood grown in sustainable forests. The manufacturing processes conform to the environmental regulations of the country of origin.

ISBN: 978-1-78243-003-2 in hardback print format
ISBN: 978-1-78243-004-9 in trade paperback format
ISBN: 978-1-78243-019-3 in EPub format
ISBN: 978-1-78243-020-9 in Mobipocket format

1 2 3 4 5 6 7 8 9 10

Designed and typeset by Design 23, London
Printed and bound by CPI Group (UK) Ltd, Croydon, CR0 4YY

www.mombooks.com

Contents

Foreword

Will's single 'Reach for the Stars' is, on its surface, about space travel. With its grand, orchestral opening it has an iconic, Hollywood feel from the start. It was chosen to become the first song to be played on Mars, its cleverly named 'universal premiere' taking place in August 2012. The song's significance in Will's story goes beyond that though – its lyrics almost reflect the mission statement that has guided his life. He has always refused to accept that the sky is the limit, and the personal universe he operates within has always been a vast arena.

Whatever he has achieved in his life, he has responded to each achievement by aiming ever higher. Even his clothing range, deliberately evocative of an intergalactic superhero, fits with the song's science-fiction atmosphere. His life story to date also tallies with the title of the song in another sense: a ravenous and successful networker, Will has reached for many stars for collaboration and discovered – to his delight

– that many were only too happy to meet his grasp.

And the public, it seems, is no less attracted to him. Why does he enchant us so?

The answer can be found, in part, in the way he runs against the grain of twenty-first-century celebrity culture. In an age in which people can become famous with precious little talent or justification, Will's abilities shine. Although still in his thirties, in addition to his role as frontman of the planet-conquering supergroup The Black Eyed Peas, he has proven himself to be a fine solo artist; a distinguished and in-demand producer; a manager; actor; designer; businessman and philanthropist. He is also a popular reality-television coach, thanks to his memorable presence on the first series of BBC One's primetime Saturday night TV show *The Voice*.

He has approached all of his endeavours with only the highest success in mind. In his autobiography, *Fallin' Up*, his Black Eyed Peas bandmate, Taboo, summed-up Will's approach to life well, 'He never walked on the playing field to be a participant, he walked on with a desire to be the greatest. Number one. Unrivalled. That was the pressure he exerted on himself. Always.' If he has not deserved his fame through all these channels of activity, it is hard to see how he ever will. He has earned a substantial personal fortune. The scale of it is disputed but it is generally believed to be not far either side of £50 million.

There is more to his appeal than all that, though. Will's admirers love his relentless positivity, particularly as he has come to their attention during such uncertain and unsettling times. Since the turn of the century, the threat of terror, renewed global tensions, environmental turmoil and the economic downturn have left the public keen for messages of hope and encouragement. Indeed, it is no coincidence that Will played such a large part in the 2008 election campaign for Barack Obama. The Democrat leader's slogans of positivity and hope chimed deep within Will's own psyche. Will also forms a refreshing, some might say old-fashioned contrast to the tendency of many modern celebrities to 'over-share' their personal peccadilloes and dramas to an almost grotesque degree. Will's mysterious private life intrigues us – all the more so due to the enthusiasm with which many of his contemporaries air their every dirty garment in public. Indeed, even his catchy stage name of 'will.i.am' serves as a veil between the real Will and the public: removing that veil is difficult yet rewarding.

In the pages ahead we will explore the differences between will.i.am and William James Adams Jr, and where one begins and the other ends. Until now, his private life has mostly been an enigma, and that suits him just fine. He is a stranger to scandal in large part because he rarely allows himself enough spare time to get into any scrapes. Pressed by a newspaper journalist over why he did not – as far as the public is concerned – have a girlfriend, Will said: 'I'm too busy turning my dreams into reality.' It was a slightly self-aggrandizing reply, an evasive one even, but it was no less truthful for that. In common with a growing number of twenty-first-century celebrities, Will has built a life for himself into which a significant other would find it hard to fit. Work and creativity always come first.

Indeed, while it is a comparison that neither man may enjoy after they fell out over the role of Will's client Cheryl Cole in the American series of *The X Factor*, Will's personal life can be understood to a large extent by comparing it with that of Simon Cowell. Both men are tireless workaholics who are so busy and industrious that they have little time to fully mourn their lack of a consistent 'significant other'. A more influential similarity between the men is one that makes their chances of settling down in the future unlikely: both are beautifully hopeless mummy's boys. Will can scarcely complete an interview with the media without praising his mother, Debra. When he wants to praise someone, he does so by comparing them with Debra. He values her advice even as he approaches his forties. He might never meet a woman who he will admire more than his mother; a large part of him does not want to.

Like all true eccentrics, he seems blissfully unaware of what an eccentric he is. The kookiness of his dress, lifestyle and language all come naturally to him. It is little surprise that longstanding Anglophile Will is fast becoming an honorary Englishman: indeed he is like a rapping, African-American twist on the classic, eccentric English gentleman. Boy, can he talk: he has been described as 'a quote monster'. A loquacious, fast-talking and fast-thinking man, he never knowingly under talks. Annabel Rivkin, who interviewed him for *ES* magazine, recalled how his 'verbal floodgates fly open and all of a sudden he's on a manifesto-centric roll, holding forth, twitchy, lyrical, cheeky. It's over-stimulating stuff.' Another writer described an encounter with him as 'frazzling', and 'mildly exhausting'.

Sometimes, though, he is more concise. Asked which phrase he uses too often, Will quickly identified his favourite one. Keen viewers of *The Voice*, who noted with growing amusement how often he used the slang term 'dope' (meaning good; great), will be surprised that he does not consider that his most over-used saying. Instead, the words Will just cannot stop using are: 'That's crazy.' Perhaps when he does use that phrase, he is reflecting not just on the moment, but on his whole life story.

1 Reaching New Heights

In 2006, the Black Eyed Peas were visiting an impoverished neighbourhood in Soweto, South Africa, when the band became surrounded by kids. Lifting the arm of a fourteen-year-old boy, Will told the excitable ensemble, 'He is fourteen. When I was fourteen, I started a group that became the Black Eyed Peas. I, too, came from a poor background. But I have made it – and so can you!'

His positive energy and powers of inspiration have been noted, lauded and enjoyed by many. Will believes he inherited them from the person who inspires *him* more than anyone: his mother, Debra. 'She's supermom and also my best friend,' he told the *Sun*. 'I love her. You should see the text messages she sends me.' One such message read, 'No matter how successful you are, we are still struggling.' Will described messages such as that from his mother as 'like an ego smack – great reminders of where you are from and where you are in the world. Mom made me think anything was possible.' The struggle that his mother alludes to is real, and Will's positivity cannot conceal the challenges he has been through from the start of his life.

People often ask him which nationality he is. His answer is very simple: 'I'm an American.' For him, the commonplace description 'African American' is not an option. 'When you ask the black guy in Brazil what nationality he is, he doesn't say, "African Brazilian",' reasoned Will in *O* magazine. 'He says, "Brazilian". Someone doesn't say, "I'm African English". They're English.' Will knows his ancestors came from Africa but he does not know from which part of the continent they hail, so he prefers to consider himself simply American, 'the way jazz and blues are American music. The way peach cobbler is an American dessert.' His choices of imagery reflect a kooky dimension to his love of America – and indeed to much of his life. Will is not acting when he comes across this way: he is an authentic eccentric.

He was born on 15 March 1975, and that year, the world he was born into was twisting to a soundtrack dominated by Bruce Springstreen's 'Born in the USA', *Jaws, The Godfather Part II and One Flew Over the Cuckoo's Nest* were the big movies of the year, and Muhammad Ali was in his ascendancy in the boxing ring. It was also a significant year in terms of American foreign policy: the Vietnam War came to an end and the US pulled out of Cambodia. President

Gerald Ford was in the White House.

His date of birth makes Will a Pisces. He is a keen believer in many spiritual and esoteric trends, and astrology is one of them. As he knows, among the many positive traits associated with Pisceans are adaptability, devotion and imagination. Whether or not one shares his belief in astrology, it is clear that Will has displayed each of these characteristics. Compassion is another virtue with which Pisceans are linked. As we shall see, Will has also shown plenty of that. Less positive characteristics Pisceans are said to portray include over-sensitiveness, indecision and laziness. But even Will's fiercest critics would struggle to build a case that the restless, workaholic Will is in any way lazy, even emotionally. Indeed, his sensitive nature is clear, and is perhaps the price that he pays for such a creative and imaginative mind.

He was born and raised in east Los Angeles, in a district called Boyle Heights. The impoverished, rough neighbourhood in which he grew up created hardships for Will, but it would also provide rich inspiration for his future creative work in the Black Eyed Peas and beyond. For instance, the fact his was the only black family in the area continues to resonate with Will to this day. How could that band ever have convincingly rocked the 'misfit' image, had its pivotal member not grown up as an outsider himself?

The project he lived in was called Estrada Court. Will, who has never met his father, was raised by his mother, Debra, in a large family. Debra has four biological children and ultimately adopted another four kids. 'I have two brothers and a sister, and Mom adopted two other girls when they were infants; then she just recently adopted two other boys, who are six and seven,' he told the *Guardian*. Will's father, a maintenance worker called William Sr, had left the family between Will's conception and birth. Before Will himself could escape the Estrada Court Housing Project physically, he did his best to do so emotionally. We all love to dream as children. Will still does: 'You get to mould your reality. If I didn't mould my reality then I'd still be in the ghetto where people like me are supposed to stay. You have to dream your way out of the nightmare.'

He had plenty to escape from: not just the material poverty but also the emotional issues that arise in single-parent households. Reports have found that children in single-parent families are five times more likely to develop emotional problems than those living with both parents. They are also three times as likely to become aggressive or badly behaved. Will's essentially good behaviour as a child is therefore all the more to be admired.

Also present in the family house were other members of the clan, as Elizabeth Gutierrez, a childhood friend of Will, explained to the *Mirror*. Pointing at the house the family lived in, she said: 'Will lived there with his grandmother Sarah, mother, Debra, his two uncles, an aunt and some siblings. They were the only black family here – everyone else is Mexican. They didn't have much money, no one around here does. But they were really nice.' Indeed, for Will, his strong, and 'really nice' family helped keep him happy despite their humble surroundings. The love simply transcended any tests that were thrown at them. 'For me, with my mum and my family and my upbringing … it was heaven,' he told the *Guardian*. 'It was wonderful, because of my family.' Also weighing-in to his upbringing were four uncles: 'my Uncle Donnie, my Uncle Rendal Fay, my Uncle Lynn, my Uncle Roger. Those are my mother's brothers. Not the Smothers Brothers.'

We all fantasize both about magical futures and also parallel presents. For Will, the need to imagine other worlds was especially keen, as his reality was tough and stark. In some interviews, he has been far less romantic about his childhood than he was in the chat with the *Guardian* mentioned above. It was a rough neighbourhood: 'There were a lot of gangs. A lot of my friends are dead, were in prison, on drugs or were selling drugs.'

To this day, Will feels relief that he did not meet such a fate himself. How he did so is little mystery to him, as he simply followed one of the two respectable paths he felt were open to him. 'You either joined the gang or you did arts or sports,' he continued. 'My attire got me through, though. The louder you dressed, it became obvious that you were not in a gang.' As we shall see, the legacy of this 'hard-knock' childhood showed up in other ways when he began to make his fortune later in life. It would make it hard for him to understand the intricacies of his finances. 'When you are from the ghetto there is no financial literacy,' he said.

Nowadays, Will spends a lot of his time in England, where he found a parallel neighbourhood that reminded him of Boyle Heights. Surprisingly, this was not in an inner-city region of London, Manchester or another metropolis. Instead, he found England's equivalent of Boyle Heights in Somerset of all places. Will ran through the area during his mile with the Olympic torch in 2012. 'There's one area, it's like a village of houses and it looked like the neighbourhood I came from in Boyle Heights, where the neighbours looked after the neighbours, and it looked like a real community and that reminded me of the community I come from,' he said afterwards, to the amusement of some in both Britain and America. Despite the picture of neighbourly co-operation Will paints, the harsher realities of his life remained hard to ignore.

At the same time as he was enduring those realities, his future Black Eyed Peas bandmates were also experiencing hardships of their own. Indeed, the childhoods of the band would shape the bond they would later form. Will's bandmate, Taboo, for instance, has estimated that 'sixty per cent' of the 'hood' in which he grew up were gangsters. He recalls going to sleep to a soundtrack of violent 'bedlam' in the parking lot, and has also written of the ever-present smell of cannabis that he describes as 'this scent of childhood'. As Will had done, Taboo watched his mother work 'her ass off' to provide for the family. Will is in no sense angry or bitter as a result of the challenges of his childhood. 'I'm pretty blessed to be able to share all those experiences, from living around Mexicans to going to church with all black people,' Will told the *Phoenix New Times*. 'I don't look at it as, "Wow, I'm the only one – fuck you." I look at it as, "Wow, I'm blessed to be able to relate".' The reader who appreciates such examples of people turning a challenge or setback into a positive will find much to enjoy in the pages and chapters ahead.

*

The first school Will attended was an hour's bus ride away from the family home. It was called Paul Revere Junior School, named after the famous American patriot, and it provided the building blocks for the education of a future American star. He enjoyed reading, particularly the series produced by one of children's fiction's most enduring authors. 'I liked Dr Seuss,' he told *The New York Times*. Even as young as nine years of age, Will was not only falling in love with music, nor was he only dreaming of a future career in the music industry – he was actively working towards making that goal come true. In fact, as far as Will was concerned, it was not a dream or a goal, but an inevitability. He was going to succeed. To that end, he experimented in his room, recording himself singing and rapping over backing tracks. As well as honing his vocal skills, he was also trying to learn how music production worked.

One track he 'produced' as a kid was of him rapping over the Bob Dylan track 'Forever Young'. (Later in life he would follow the same path for a Pepsi promotion.) He also practised dance moves, honing the various skills he knew he would need to succeed. So it was early in life, then, that Will's hyperactivity surfaced. Indeed, he was diagnosed – formally or informally, we do not know which – with attention deficit hyperactivity disorder (ADHD). 'Yeah, when I was a kid, they said I had ADD, or whatever,' he told the *Radio Times*. 'They said I was hyper. ADHD? AHHD? Whatever. That's cool. Actually, I've made it work for the best for me. And my mom encouraged me in everything I did.'

Indeed she did. At the age of ten, Will got to see a new kind of life after being given a significant opportunity when his mother sent him to school in a wealthy neighbourhood near Pacific Palisades. The Magnet Program, designed to offer specialized educational opportunities to children from any part of society, regardless of family income or background, helped ease his passage to a better school in a better area.

In Los Angeles there's a saying: If you're famous you live in the Hollywood Hills, if you're rich you live in Beverly Hills, and if you're lucky you live in Pacific Palisades. Will must have felt lucky indeed as he arrived in this area each morning: the contrast between it and Boyle Heights is striking. Despite the accuracy of the saying about the district, the reality is slightly more complicated. Famous and rich people do live in Pacific Palisades, but they are often down-to-earth celebrities, those who do not buy into the game of hiding behind literal, metaphorical and brickwork sunglasses. This is a district in which accomplished people live a normal, albeit comfortable, existence. Famous names who have lived there include Ben Affleck, Larry David, Jamie Lee Curtis, Ray Liotta, Ozzy Osbourne and Steven Spielberg. This opened Will's eyes to the possibilities that fame and fortune can bring. Summing up the difference between where he lived and where he studied, Will told an audience of British students that the gap was: 'Culture-wise and distance ... like sending a kid from London to France for school.'

The sense of opportunity and its rich reward is strong in the neighbourhood, which is little short of heavenly in some parts. It is difficult not to be inspired and enlivened. It was, therefore, a significant moment when his mother decided to send Will there. 'She wanted me to be challenged,' he explained. One of the challenges was raised by the demographics of his school. He went from being the only black boy in a predominantly Latino neighbourhood to being the only black boy in a predominantly white school.

The establishment he attended was called the Palisades Charter High School. For him, the basic truth about this area was the most pertinent: 'it isn't a ghetto'. It would turn out to be a fateful moment in his life story. However, more immediately these were long days for Will. He would be waiting for the school bus just after 6 a.m. each day, which meant he sometimes missed breakfast. 'And when you're on food stamps and lunch tickets, missing breakfast is not good for a kid,' he told the *Financial Times*. He was a member of the school choir and an enthusiastic participator in other extra-curricular activities, so Will rarely returned home until 8 p.m. Looking back on the opportunity, Will is not one to complain. Without the Magnet Program, he said, he 'would never have seen what the world was like … I would be stuck thinking the world was the five miles of my surrounding area.'

Comparing the wealthy neighbourhood he travelled to for his schooling, and the ghetto district in which he grew up, Will sensed that in the latter area, the encouragement to disaster was almost inevitable. 'There's a family of influences that dictate behaviour,' he told the *Financial Times*. 'In the ghetto, there's a liquor store, a cheque-cashing place and a motel. What that tells you psychologically is: get a cheque, cash it. Take a couple of steps. Buy some liquor and get drunk, go home and get kicked out of your house. And here's a place to sleep along the way.' In contrast, he said, in richer areas the set-up encourages more positive behaviour. He was learning plenty at school, yet Will's education was also self-administered – merely by keeping his eyes open and his wits about him at all times.

Former classmates of Will remember him as a charismatic and charming boy. Yvette Bucio told the *Mirror*: 'I used to ride the bus with Will or "Willy" as we called him. He was exactly the same then as he is now – stylish, attractive and charming. He used to get along with everybody whether they were white, black, Mexican or whatever. After he left, he wrote next to my picture in the yearbook that he had a crush on me. I was really flattered. But then I found out he did the same to all the girls.' It seems he was quite the amiable politician even back then. Quite the singer, too: Angelica Pereyra, another former classmate of Will's, recalled how he began freestyle rapping contests in the playground. The boy who would later appear as a judge on a talent contest was a skilled organizer. 'He was great and everyone used to gather round him and start cheering and shouting,' said Pereyra. 'The teachers would always run over because they thought a fight was going on.' Instead, what they were witnessing were the first live performances from a boy who would later sell out the world's biggest stadiums and arenas.

Meanwhile, as his adolescence continued, Will's sexual awakening was beginning. Given the element of mystery that has long surrounded his romantic life, the origins of it are fascinating. Naturally, those origins are less than straightforward, too. As a teenager he fantasized about Charo, the flamboyant and vivacious Latina television personality. She had already been famous for the best part of a decade when she first came to young Will's attention in the early 1980s. With her trademark saying 'cuchi-cuchi' – often accompanied by a sassy wiggle of her hips – Charo caught the attention of many males. 'I loved me some Charo,' Will told *Elle* magazine. 'Back in the 80s, she was everywhere – *The Love Boat, Fantasy Island*.' He says he enjoyed watching her wherever she appeared.

Will's sexuality is the subject of mystery and conjecture. By his own admission, his introduction to sex was unconventional. When the subject of masturbation was alluded to by one interviewer, Will offered the information that: 'I didn't do that until I was nineteen.' So, while his male school friends will undoubtedly have been exploring themselves enthusiastically, Will refrained from doing so until he was comfortably into manhood. Asked why, he replied: 'I think my mom had a big role in it. It was a subject we never talked about growing up.' Stranger still was that he hinted that he had lost his virginity a year before, when he was eighteen. It was a less than romantic experience as he describes it: 'her mother was in the other room; it was horrible. And then she cheated on me. But I stayed with her, like a bonehead.'

Will's explanation that his mother's lack of commentary about sex as she raised him was responsible for his abstinence is intriguing. It is hard to not speculate that there must be more to it, though. Few mothers, after all, would discuss the subject regularly, even at all, with their children. Perhaps he is, cryptically or even subconsciously, referring more to the absence of a father figure. Without an authoritative male voice to discuss the birds and the bees with him, it seems he learned about sex and romance more delicately than he might have. 'Because I was raised around girls, I think I've adopted that perspective on sex,' he has admitted.

Even back then, Will was living around the rules that his mother constructed for his relationships with girls. 'She was real strict, but she could be lenient,' he told the *Guardian*. 'I couldn't bring girls in the house but she let me talk on the phone. And my phone bill was high. I'd been with my first girlfriend, Carmen Perez, for three months before she kissed me. I told my ma, who was like, "I didn't send you to school to be acting mannish".' She had, it seems, somewhat delicate expectations for her son.

Delicate is not, however, a word that can be used to describe all elements of his development. There were some harsh punishments meted out at home. His mother told him: 'I am your daddy.' She was as good as her word, inflicting physical punishment when she felt it necessary. For instance, when he was at high school, Will developed a habit of scrawling graffiti. He used to write the word 'expo' – an abbreviation of exposure – on walls and other surfaces. The thrill of graffiti has never quite left Will. In later life he would be caught by the police, but back at high school it was his Uncle Fay who busted him. He duly reported Will to his mother, saying: 'Debra! Willie over there writing on them walls!' Debra was furious. She called Will into the house and told him: 'Sit your butt down on the couch!' Will feared a formidable ticking off – but he received more than that. 'She started hitting me,' he told *Elle*.

The physical punishment certainly had the desired effect. 'My mom's discipline worked out perfectly,' he said. 'I wouldn't change a thing. And my mom got hit by my grandma, who's the sweetest person on the freakin' planet.' However, while Will is comfortable with the corporal punishment he received, he does not believe it would be as appropriate for today's children. 'Cultures change,' he said, adding that we now live in 'a different era'.

How influential has the fact Will grew up in a single-parent household been on his life? Later, while in the throes of a less-than-perfect eight-year relationship with a woman, Will saw a counsellor and was encouraged to conclude that the absence of a father in his upbringing had left a specific mark on his mentality. 'I learned in counselling that me and my ex-girlfriend both have a fear of abandonment from not having a role model in relationships,' he told the *Guardian*. 'My mom's never been married. I've never even seen my mom kiss a dude.' That said, Will is the first to say that his mother was a pivotal influence in the success he would go on to achieve professionally. She encouraged him to be different, primarily in order to give him the best chance possible to ascend from the tough surroundings in which he'd been raised.

However, her motivation was wider than that. She wanted

Will to explore himself and be an individual regardless of the circumstances of his childhood. His was not an upbringing in which unimaginative conformity was automatically valued or rewarded. Nor was undue deference: Debra wanted Will to be a leader rather than a follower. This wish showed itself in a number of ways during his childhood. For instance, rather than encouraging him to join in with the games other kids played, Debra showed him how much more value there was in creating his own games, so other kids would come and join him.

It was during the first half of his teenage years that Will began to experiment with making music. '[It was] when I was like thirteen, fifteen,' he said. 'At thirteen, I started rhyming. At fifteen, I started making beats.' Also, at the age of fourteen, he began to learn about how to write his own music. His reasoning was that if you wanted to move to Germany, you would learn German first. Therefore, if you wanted to move into the music industry, you had to learn music.

Which was something he was continuing to do. Before he was will.i.am, Will was Will 1X (sometimes spelled as WilloneX). It is not quite such a catchy moniker, but it represents where he was at this stage in his life. Indeed, according to someone who knew Will at the time, this earlier character was a 'mini-me' reflection of the iconic will.i.am celebrity of today.

One of his childhood friends was Stefan Gordy. The son of Motown founder Berry Gordy, Stefan would go on to achieve musical fame himself later in life, as 'Redfoo', one of the members of the band LMFAO. Will first noticed him when he realized, with amusement, that Stefan would arrive at school wearing tennis kit.

At this stage, Will was using his younger sister's talking bear to record some rudimentary raps. 'I used to record on my little sister's Teddy Ruxpin tapes to make Teddy Ruxpin rap,' he told the *Huffington Post*. 'So I used to put my little demo inside his belly and press play and he used to kick my lyrics in homeroom show-and-tell.' To take the recording further, he leveraged his relationship with Stefan. 'So after homeroom show-and-tell, I gave the tape to Stefan: "Give this to your pops". And he didn't give it to his dad, so he gave it to his brother, Kerry, and then Kerry says, "You're really talented, this is cool."' This was enough for Will to impose renewed hustling pressure on Stefan. 'To make a long story short, in the tenth grade I tell Stefan, "Tell your daddy to get you some music equipment so we can record after school".'

While studying at a summer school at John Marshall High in Los Feliz, Will first met another boy who would change his life. Allan Pineda Lindo, now better known as apl.de.ap (or simply apl), of The Black Eyed Peas, quickly struck up a rapport with Will. Allan was born in the Philippines to a Filipino mother and black father. His father left home soon after Allan was born, leaving Allan's mother to raise seven children on her own. Although he was the youngest of the family, Allan quickly grew an old head on his young shoulders. His family was struggling to survive and so even as a child he worked on a local farm to bring some much needed extra funds into the household. His grace was rewarded when a television commercial, made by a charity called the Pearl Buck Foundation, featured his plight on American television. A Californian businessman was so moved by the commercial that he arranged to adopt the fourteen-year-old and bring him to a new, more comfortable, life in Los Angeles. It was that man, Joe Ben Hudgens – a former roommate of one of Will's uncles – who set in motion the wheels that would bring Lindo to Will's attention.

So Will began to write songs with apl and they quickly developed an understanding that was so strong that, to outsiders observing their creative interactions, it appeared almost telepathic. This synergy would make them very rich in the years ahead. For the time being, it provided them with something valuable in a different way: a sense of exciting hope. Will was learning quickly the methodology behind a good song and he soon realized that writing lyrics from personal experience was the best route to a powerful song. He also tended to eschew the use of long words, feeling that simplicity was key to the creation of a catchy message. However, the lyrics were not the part of the composition he generally started with, because he also lived by the rule: rhythm comes first, words later. Indeed, his style of songwriting quickly developed a regular sequence, which lasted into the formation of the Black Eyed Peas. Taboo, who would also be a member of that band, described it as: 'rhythm-became-mumbles-became-words-became-lyrics-became song'.

As well as hanging out at club nights such as Club What?, Will began to attend raves in Los Angeles. Alongside a childhood friend called Pasquale (Pasquale Rotella, now the boss of Insomniac Events and architect of the annual electronic dance music festival Electric Daisy Carnival), he partied the nights away at some huge and thrilling events.

Will, quite the technology buff nowadays as we shall see, has looked back fondly on the movement around these parties. At the time they seemed to be cutting edge but now elements of their organization seem quaint. 'In LA in the early, early 1990s, there were raves that were like secret clubs, and thousands of people would go, and the way you found out about it was you went to a map point and the map point gave you another map point and that map point gave you directions,' he said, during a conversation with the *LA Times*. 'Way before pagers, way before cell phones and the Internet. You physically had to go to two locations to get the address. Tens of thousands of people would show up in the desert or in the warehouses or these secret locations where the raves would be.'

These were exciting events with thronging attendances. 'There would be, you know, between 10,000 and 50,000 people,' he told the *Guardian*. 'People would express themselves with loud colours, DJs would play crazy beats,' he added. Asked whether these gatherings were legal or not, he admitted they were not. '[They were] illegal, yes, all right, OK, you got me there,' he said. 'We were kids!'

It is worth restating that Will was still a schoolboy as he and Pasquale partied the night away at these raves. He was, in fact, a tenth-grade pupil. The morning after one of these raves, he and his classmates would be discussing their night out as they sat down in the classroom. He remembers whispering with classmates about how 'crazy' a night out had been, and a classmate turning round to tell him: 'Dude, I'm still rolling.'

Will admits that other kids at his school took drugs at these raves, though he denies he did. 'I'm talking about eleventh-graders, fifteen-year-olds in high school,' he said. 'Where I was going to high school people were rolling, and coming down from the drug. I didn't do that stuff, and Pasquale didn't do that stuff. But we went, and we liked the vibe and the scene.'

That vibe and scene captured Will's imagination in such a way that it has, at the time of writing at least, yet to release its grip. The rave scene quickly peaked and, in its most exciting and authentic form, disappeared. However, some acts have kept the flame alive by incorporating its light into their own material. The Black Eyed Peas are one of those bands. More immediately, back then, these nights out were great ways for Will to release any tension inside him. His teenage troubles seemed to melt away as he danced.

He was also paying close attention to the music coming out of his radio at the time. He noted the way that hip-hop was up-tempo in this era, and the influence that this had on rave culture. Songs such as 'It Takes Two', which he clocked in at 127 beats per minute, and Jungle Brothers, Technotronic and Queen Latifah tracks that added a 'poppier' sound to the mix, all fed into the prevailing atmosphere. 'And we liked that because that's what we danced to,' he told the *LA Times*, describing him and his friends at the time as 'what you called "house dancers" – we used to dance house.'

The next phase was when Will and his fellow house dancers – we are here effectively describing the Black Eyed Peas and their entourage before the band was officially formed – moved a step further. This started when Will and Allan Lindo began to perform together around Los Angeles. A fellow student named Dante Santiago sometimes joined them for these performances. They called themselves Atban Klann, and during one of their performances, they were to be noticed by a highly revered figure on the rap scene.

Born with the less-than-gangster name of Eric Lynn Wright, Eazy-E would grow-up to be so influential he would be declared the 'the Godfather of Gangsta Rap'. He formed a label, Ruthless Records, and then a band – N.W.A. (Niggaz With Attitude). His band would prove to be a huge hit, practically defining the gangsta rap movement in the eyes of millions around the world in the late 1980s and early 1990s. While the band remained a controversial one due to their name and many of their lyrics, songs such as 'Express Yourself' made for a more mainstream and positive dimension to their act. Meanwhile, Eazy-E scouted for new acts to sign to Ruthless Records. One of them would be Will. 'I was free-styling at a club event that David Faustino from *Married With Children* was hosting, and there were some Ruthless Records representatives there,' Will explained later in an interview with the AV Club website. It was an arrangement entirely free of red tape, which suited him at first. 'They signed me just off my free-styling. Once again, there were no contracts, no demo, no lawyers, or any of that dumb shit. I got fucked in the long run, but it started out well.'

He received $10,000 for his agreement on the deal, but the prestige and boost it gave him were immeasurable. He even began ghostwriting lyrics for Eazy-E. 'I knew how to write those kind of rhymes, I just didn't want to rap,' he said. 'Eazy-E was one of those cats that wanted to have dope MCs around him to write his shit, or to just be there. He just wanted to be surrounded by dope shit. Now, I'm not saying that I was one of his dope-shit selections, but he wasn't closed-minded, that guy.'

The credibility that this deal lent Will can't be overestimated. As a schoolboy he had been noted by one of the leading rap artists of the moment. 'I was in high school, so it was a dream come true,' he said in an interview with *Hip-Hop DX*. 'To be in the eleventh grade, twelfth grade, and you're running with Eazy. N.W.A. was, still … think about what they were in '92, '93. That was unbelievable. That's like being in high school right now, and you're working with … you can't compare it. You can't compare it to 50 Cent or Jay-Z, because Eazy-E was the first nigga.'

He later recalled how he showed off about his success. 'I come to school with a record deal, like, "Yo, I got a record deal, ten G's",' he added. 'To a seventeen-year-old, ten thousand dollars – granted, it was, like, for life, Eazy-E had me signed like for ever.'

Will wanted to confirm the faith that was increasingly being placed in him and so he began to take part in 'rapping battles' at a nightclub called Ballistyx. It was there that he and apl first met their future bandmate, Taboo, putting the seal on the initial line-up of what would become the Black Eyed Peas.

It was a friend of Will's, known as Mooky, who suggested that he meet up with Taboo. Will remembered seeing Taboo – whose real name is Jaime Luis Gómez – as he was dancing or, in their words, 'doing something special'. Wearing 'thrift' clothes, complete with a beret, Taboo made for quite a sight. 'He's kind of scary looking, but his dancing is dope,' apl told Will. Soon, both men began to wonder: 'Who's the dancer?'

As for Taboo, he remembered seeing a sixteen-year-old 'eccentric-looking black dude', who was 'rapping like a madman'. As Will rapped he played with his dreadlocks. His 'wide-eyed intensity' made Taboo wonder if this eccentric was 'in some kind of trance'. Will was rapping faster than Taboo had ever heard anyone rap before. It was a 'whirlwind', remembered Will's future bandmate in his autobiography. Even then, Will's charisma and stage-presence were powerful. He 'owned the floor' and had more energy than the rest of the club combined. 'He was as colourful as his socks were loud, and as brilliant as anything I'd seen on the street, in videos, or in battles.'

From the moment the three band members first got together as a unit, recalls Taboo, it was clear they shared a 'unity in spirit, intention and meaning'. He recalls liking Will, who he viewed as 'a perfectionist, all about the pristine clothes, the focus to be number one, and keen on detail'. However, that perfectionism could flare-up into confrontation with anyone he felt might be poised to upstage him. During an open-mic battle with a twelve-year-old called Little E, Will at first let the youngster have his moment on the stage. Then, Will's competitive spirit kicked in and he fiercely contested. 'Will turned it on and smoked him,' recalled Taboo. Will's performance made him the clear winner of the battle. Afterwards, the boy's uncle confronted the triumphant winner, accusing him of 'disrespecting my little nephew'. Voices were raised and the men began to shove each other. Will's friend Mooky had to step in to prevent violence breaking out.

Will was proving to be an unstoppable force in these MC battles. As the Hollywood MC champion he managed a winning streak of weekly victories that ran for an astonishing eighteen months. He seemed almost invincible – and certainly felt it at times. He even saw off a highly rated MC from Chicago, called Twista, an artist who had appeared in *The Guinness Book of World Records* as the fastest rapper in the world. As Taboo put it, 'hip hop greats were bowing down' to Will.

There was no doubting the ferocity of Will's ambitions. Taboo recalls how Will used to talk about his 'big dream' and how he was going to make it work. He was a good talker even then: Taboo describes how Will was a natural-born storyteller, who was 'fast, clever and animated'. Although he could be shy and 'guarded' when he first met people as a teenager, Will would soon open up once he knew someone – and as he opened up, he revealed huge reserves of determination, vision and ability. Few who met him left after an encounter with Will unaware that he intended to go places in life and that he had the ability to do so. His energy was such that he did not only impress people with his own ambition: he also recharged their own aspirations and positivity. He quite naturally had the sort of charisma and presence that politicians sometimes spend enormous sums to try to develop.

According to Taboo, Will was also an expert roller of joints. In his book, Taboo remembers Will handing him 'the most expertly, perfectly rolled joint' he had ever seen – he described it as such a finely formed cigarette that it was as if Will had 'micromanaged' its construction. What also impressed Taboo was that the joint had been rolled so quickly – but then Will has long lived his life as if he is late for an important meeting with lots of other ambitious eccentrics. Not that Will was a pot-smoker himself. According to his bandmate, having had a bad experience with the drug, Will had decided never to try it again – and it seems clear that he has abstained from drug-taking. Perhaps he felt that cannabis, which has a reputation as a drug that saps its users of energy, focus, belief and ambition, was the last thing he needed, as he was positively overflowing with all those virtues. As Taboo said, Will emitted an 'invincible aura that screamed: "I'm going to be somebody".' Even the way Will dressed, Taboo said, absolutely shone with 'fire and hunger'. Extensive cannabis use would surely dampen that ardour.

*

When he was twenty, Will fell in love for the first time. It was an association that developed into an eight-year-long relationship, and not one that was entirely enjoyable. During the relationship, when 'things got hard', the couple even went to a relationship counsellor, who encouraged them to do activities together. One of these was to cook food together – 'that's why I know how to cook now', said Will, looking back. 'It wasn't abusive, it was just destructive emotionally.' He has been coy about the identity of the woman, only saying: 'she still lives in the ghetto we came from, in Compton, LA', and that: 'she doesn't care about entertainment, or fashion, she's just a real person'.

As a result, the more famous Will became while they were together, the more uninterested she became in the world of celebrity. While Will appreciated her lack of interest in fame, the two were pulling in different directions. Their split was inevitable but, even after it, Will felt that what they had would, in a sense, last for ever. 'I will always love my ex-girlfriend,' he later told the *Guardian*. 'She'll get married, but that love we had, regardless of exclusivity, is beyond that. Love lasts for ever.' He would even go on to offer her a slice of the profits from one of the songs she inspired.

Some of Will's views on sex and sexuality have been highly controversial. He has, more recently, made some rather prim and prudish statements about it, and it is worth briefly stepping forward in the story to connect them. He was asked what would guarantee to put him off a woman. 'If she had condoms in her house, that would just fuckin' throw me off,' he said. 'That's just tacky.' Some women found this statement highly offensive. At the time, his female interviewer took him up on his outburst, asking him why he was so offended by the thought of a woman taking precautions. 'I just think, like, if you're into someone and you guys get to that level, then that's something you should converse about together and say, "Hey, maybe we should get some",' he said.

Outraged women asked who he thought he was to suggest there was something wrong with them having contraceptives. Others felt his views were arcane or misogynistic. However they really seem to hint at the contradictions that make Will such an intriguing character. As far as some of his fans are concerned, his contradictions and complexities survive to this day – they are what make Will such a vulnerable, and therefore attractive, character.

Even before he was famous, Will was building a reputation for himself not only as a promising musician and performer, but also as an attractive character of dazzling influence. Together, these gifts would take him far. It was his mother who continued to influence him as he formed his musical energies into a three-piece unit, into a successful band, then fashioned that into a world-conquering supergroup. 'My mom keeps me down to earth,' he said. 'I'd hate for my mom to see me act like a dick, so I try not to act like a dick.' Not that he would use such language in front of Debra. As he told *The New York Times*: 'When I get around my mom, all my cuss words are deleted from my vocabulary. Automatically, they just leave.'

It was Debra's example that lit the spark to the forcefield of motivational charisma that has come to serve Will so well. She was the first to lift him from the surroundings he was born into. First, she did so emotionally, by encouraging him to stay positive and not fall into the many traps that surrounded them. Then she did so by arranging for him to be schooled in a better area. Will has honoured her in many ways, not least the fact that rather than writing songs that glorified the squalor and danger that surrounded him, he instead wrote positive songs that encouraged everyone, whatever their background, to believe in themselves, to better themselves and to enjoy the ride. In so doing, he not only honoured Debra, he also put a smile on faces around the world.

2 Building a Band

One day, a momentous meeting took place when Will and Taboo met in the studio car park. As well as being significant in the history of the band that became the Black Eyed Peas, this meeting is also pertinent to understanding Will's own powerfully alluring charm. Prior to the formation of the Black Eyed Peas, Taboo had been in a band called Pablo, and he had found himself growing increasingly disgruntled in the studio.

Taboo's memories of what happened next do much to shed light on the power of Will's positive charisma. He recalled that when Will fixed you in eye-to-eye contact, the energy he could communicate was immense. Taboo said that even when Will was a teenager, his eyes could 'hook you and plug you' into his own vast reserves of self-belief. His charisma was also matched by his compassion: Will has long been spoken of as a man with much empathy. These are the sorts of skills that jettisoned US president Bill Clinton to the White House. One wonders whether the opinionated Will might consider a crack at mainstream politics himself one day. He has stated that he will never do so, explaining: 'I'll never enter politics myself, though. I've got too many skeletons in my closet.' However, many a political career has been launched after fierce denials that the politician in question ever wanted to enter the profession. It is as if reluctance is the final stage prior to acceptance. Furthermore, in his role as the unofficial but undoubted ambassador of the band, he has shown the stature and charisma to have a good chance. America has always been open to the idea of celebrities moving into the political sphere, after all.

At this stage, three future members of the Black Eyed Peas had met each other. Will found that he had significant things in common with apl and Taboo. All three had grown up in poor families who lived in tough neighbourhoods and without the presence of a father. All three had faced difficulties, obstacles and emotional pain as a result of these disadvantages. All three had also found that in music there was a sense of salvation – and as a potential way to better themselves financially, it was a big draw. With their already heightened sense of being outsiders, they wanted to make music for other outsiders. They also felt that the right way to do this was to create positive music that lifted its listener. If only, they rightly reasoned, Will's personality and presence could be injected into the music, they would have something almost magical on their hands. The positivity was – and is – key to the Black Eyed Peas project. Will was the pivot of that positivity. He was to be at the centre of everything.

For instance, it was Will who pushed for their act to include a live band. Here again, his approach was original. He knew that the presence of a live band would take his act outside of the rap mainstream. 'I got tired of DATs and records,' he explained later. 'I wanted to allow for a certain level of human mistakes in the music. I like the idea of having a different vibe every night, you know, as to what the bass player might be feeling that night, or whatever. We just wanted live shit.'

His bandmates quickly agreed with his proposal. As Taboo commented, without a band they would resemble a 'car without wheels'. He felt this would give them the edge. So he personally assembled the musicians himself. They then set to work rehearsing in apl's garage, under Will's quasi-managerial eye. Apl loved the new intensity and freedom that the backing band gave them. 'It makes you want to be electric', he reflected. 'It gives you the freedom to move'.

By the rest of the band's admission, Will was the most focused of the line-up, with apl also particularly on the ball. As for Taboo, he described himself at that stage as a 'functioning reefer head'. It all began to make for an improbably effective ensemble.

Even through the haze of his admitted extensive cannabis use, Taboo was sharp enough to see Will's many good points. He learned a great deal from Will in the early months and years of their friendship. For instance, during the aforementioned fateful car-park encounter, when Taboo confided in Will that he was lacking confidence as a rapper. He told Will, in fact, that he felt he was 'wack at rapping'. First, Will gave Taboo a general confidence boost, stating life was not necessarily about being the best, but that the overall performance was important. Then, he offered Taboo a novel method to improve his rap technique, which involved placing a pencil in his mouth, between his teeth and behind his tongue. By rubbing his tongue against the pencil, Will created a rhythmic sound effect. He then removed the pencil from his mouth and told Taboo that he too should perform that exercise each day.

At first, Taboo, understandably, felt this was a 'shit-crazy thing to do', but such was Will's poise and confidence that Taboo was willing to try anything he suggested. 'I listened and obeyed,' said Taboo. For weeks, he would perform the pencil routine in front of the bathroom mirror each morning. Even as he did so, he would ask himself what on earth he was doing such an exercise for. Yet he persevered and he found that the speed and smoothness of his rap delivery improved very quickly. The confidence that this gave him was huge – he said his self-doubts were 'erased' by the transformation that Will's pep talk and pencil trick had prompted. This is an early, striking, example of Will's mentoring and coaching abilities. Some musicians who have gone on to become managers or talent-show judges have done so more on the strength of their celebrity, rather than their inherent suitability for a mentoring role. Will, however, has had a mentor nature for many years.

The first official recording from Atban Klann was a track entitled 'Merry Muthafuckin' Xmas'. It was released on the Eazy-E EP, *5150: Home 4 Tha Sick*, which hit the shelves on 10 December 1992. Clocking in at just under six minutes, it made for a bombastic, comedic and bawdy closer to the five-track EP. Alongside Will's band on the disc were Rudy Ray Moore, Menajahtwa and Buckwheat. The disc sold well, becoming certified gold within three months. 'So that's the first time I had a song come out,' said Will. 'That shit was dope.'

Next, the trio began working on an album. It was to be entitled *Grass Roots*. However, the album was never released in its official form – the band shelved it after tragedy struck. When Eazy-E was admitted to the Cedars Sinai Medical Center in Los Angeles, it was first assumed that he was suffering from asthma. Instead, he was diagnosed with full-blown AIDs. Having been sexually promiscuous from his early teens and having been involved in the drug world, Eazy-E had lived a life that flirted with danger.

Over the next month, he attempted to make amends with as many people as possible, but he died on 26 March 1995. Although his death was not entirely unexpected, it was a sad day for Will. Hip-hop had lost one of its most extraordinary practitioners of all time, and Will had lost the man who had given him his first leg-up into the music world.

*

Meanwhile, Will's band simply continued to evolve. Taboo's renewed confidence and ability only hastened the day when Will would invite him to join his own band. Soon, that band would be renamed from Atban Klann, to the Black Eyed Peas. It seems a wise name-change, even putting aside the benefit of hindsight. Where Atban Klann – the first word of which stands for A Tribute Beyond A Nation – is awkward to pronounce and easily forgotten, Black Eyed Peas rolls off the tongue and stays in the memory. Black Eyed Peas had been the name of Will's production company, and he simply decided to transfer it to the band. As to its origins, it had been struck upon one day when, at a brainstorming session, Will and his bandmates had been shouting out names of items that include colours. They quickly centred on 'Black Eyed Peas', the name of the bean that is popular in both the West Indies and America's south. The bean is white, with a black dot – or eye. A popular soul food, according to tradition if it is eaten at New Year one experiences a prosperous year ahead. For the band, this seemed to be a moniker that was appropriate on many levels.

Will also changed his stage name to the one the whole world knows him by now. He told *The New York Times* how he came up with his own new moniker. 'I liked playing with words,' he said. 'I noticed that my name was a sentence, meaning one with will, who is strong-willed. And so I called my mom and said, "Hey, Mom, do you mind if I call myself will.i.am?" She was like: "Whaaa? You're crazy." She was cool with it.'

The future looked bright, yet the present was glowing rather nicely as it was: something good was coming together. Both a sound and an image were being developed that matched what Will wanted. However, his ambition was broad and his bar set high. Will wanted his band to be innovators. As an example of the level of innovation he wished them to achieve, he looked to no lesser a musical icon than Michael Jackson. As well as Jacko's music itself, it was the number of 'firsts' in pop that Jackson had achieved that appealed to Will and his band. They wanted a place in both the history books and in the wider, less tangible history of broken moulds and new paths ploughed. If only Will could have known then that he would not only meet and work with Jackson one day, but that Jackson would state that he so valued Will precisely for his 'wonderful, innovative, positive and infectious' nature.

Prince was another artist that they looked to as an example of the scale of success and influence they wished to achieve. Their multicultural image was in tune with his, too. Will, apl and Taboo hoped that the narratives of their own lives would serve as part of their positive, bridge-building image. One of their first songs, called 'Joints & Jam', spoke of 'mass appeal' with 'no segregation'. It was a very 'Will' perspective on life.

One of the band's first performances as the Black Eyed Peas came at the Hollywood nightclub Grand Slam. Owned by the singer Prince, the venue had considerable symbolism and stature. Will invited Taboo to join the band ahead of the date, which he gleefully accepted. Will was so excited as he and his band arrived at the venue for their first performance, which was part of a Ruthless Records showcase evening. They pulled up outside in Will's red VW Golf, having continued their rehearsals even in the car as they drove through Los Angeles. Will told his bandmates not to be nervous. 'Just do your thing,' he told them.

Even his cool, though, was tested when the band began their set in front of the 150-strong audience. As he began to rap, someone in the audience threw an ice cube, which hit him directly in the eye – a shocking and painful experience. Rather than storm off the stage or lose his poise, though, Will turned the incident into a virtue by performing an impromptu rap about what had just happened. 'Fuck this shit – this MC just got hit,' he rhymed. As the audience's giggles turned to admiration, he added: 'But y'all can't stop my shine.'

Even as the pain in his eye worsened, Will concentrated on continuing to shine. It was a tough audience, full of 'expressionless faces', recalled Taboo, but Will soon had them enraptured. For any band line-up, let alone one performing for the first time, the legendary 'tough audience' is always a challenge. In his autobiography, Taboo recalled that the audience was 'a mean-mugging bunch of thug-like cats'. They looked the type who were more into gangsta rap-style lyrics rather than the upbeat sentiments of Will's band.

What visual spectacle were the audience confronted with? Will and apl were both wearing vintage, old-school outfits on the night. Each had long dreadlocks, too. Taboo was dressed, in his own telling, 'ninja style'. As Will continued to make a virtue of being struck by the ice, the audience got more and more onside with the band and the energy in the venue became positive. Backstage after the show, the band felt an increased bond between each other. They felt like they had become more than a band – it felt more like familial bond.

One of their next concerts was an open-air affair, at the Peace & Justice Center in *LA*. They found that the best way to test the material they were developing was in front of a live audience. Often, including at this particular concert, they would find that something that seemed a great idea when developed and performed in the garage, proved to be less of a good idea when rocked out in front of a live audience. This learning curve was a welcome development. Will in particular proved an attentive and accurate reader of an audience's mood. Even as he and his band became so enormously popular and successful in the years to come, to an extent Will continued to use audiences as 'focus groups'. For him, there is no point at which one stops seeking feedback in order to up your game. Even small concerts in the band's early days – they once played to just twenty-five people at the Florentine Gardens in Hollywood – were opportunities to test what they had been working on. In fact, he found that smaller audiences sometimes made this process easier.

There were still challenges: at their first performance in New York, Will felt that many of the audience actively 'tried' to not understand the band. He suspected that many of the audience members were MCs themselves, and as such were taking more convincing. 'If people are talking about you, you gotta live up to the hype,' he said. It was a challenge he was prepared to meet.

Will's songwriting technique began to follow a pattern from the earliest days of the band. He would find himself suddenly struck with inspiration to create a basic beat. He would quickly begin to play that beat, until a wider rhythm was born. Then the lyrics would begin to join the process. From there on, his bandmates would join in the process. These were energetic and creative sessions. The unwritten rule was that no suggestion would be mocked. As they flung ideas around, some would stick and others would not – but all were welcomed. Before they knew it, another catchy song had been created. The speed at which Will, in particular, worked was often ferocious. While his two fellow members would be writing down on paper the ideas they were working on, Will never did so. As Taboo observed, this was largely because Will's creative mind worked so fast that he would not have been able to move his pen fast enough to commit his thoughts to paper.

Slowly but surely, the band was moving up in the world. Having worked at first in a studio based in a bedroom, they moved to their first studio proper, which was based at the Loyola Marymount University, near LAX Airport. It was a thrilling moment when they first entered the studio and saw all the equipment. To Will, the hundreds of buttons and other gadgets were opportunities. For months they worked hard in the studio, generally arriving in the evening and recording until the early hours of the following morning.

Dozens of songs emerged from these sessions, including 'Fallin' Up'. The creation of this song is instructive of Will's role in the band. Apl dreamed up the chorus of the song as the band travelled by bus to a meeting. He 'freestyled' and soon more lyrics were coming to life. Later, in the studio, apl recited the lyrics to Will, also explaining the overall concept. 'Yo, that shit is dope!' Will said, and began to assemble everything needed to turn it into a proper song. He chose a Brazilian guitar riff to rework into the backing track. Full of excitement and oozing inspiration, he turned it into a fully fledged track. (Taboo would borrow the song's title for his autobiography, too.)

They proved to be enthusiastic and effective networkers. They were always on the lookout for fresh contacts in the industry. To befriend people, they found that Will was their trump card. Not only was he naturally gregarious, but also the intense stare of his eyes and his positive, creative energy, rarely failed to win people over. People would become caught up in his ambition and enthusiasm. Even those who at this stage were far more accomplished and connected than Will did not feel they could ignore him. He gave every impression of someone who was going to go far.

The next big milestone for Will to pass was signing the band to a record label – a time at which fresh bands sometimes set in stone terms that they later regret. It is a rare pop band that is anything other than keen, desperate even, for a record contract. Labels, keenly aware of that desperation, can masterfully manipulate aspiring artists into restrictive and unfair terms that are difficult to get out of. Prince, for instance, once infamously described himself as a 'slave' to his label. Sharp, cool and wise – and with his relationship with Ruthless Records a less than ideal arrangement in the long-term – Will was determined to not let his band be bullied or rushed into a deal they would later become unhappy with.

There was no shortage of takers: in 1997, several record labels had begun to hear of this new energetic and innovative band. Three in particular were taking an interest in them – Warner Bros., Sony 550 and Interscope. A showcase performance was arranged so the band could perform in front of interested label executives. It took place at the Dragonfly nightclub, on Santa Monica Boulevard in the heart of Los Angeles, the site of many such evenings in those days. The whole band knew that a great deal was at stake on the evening; however, they also believed that they deserved to succeed, and were, therefore, brimful of confidence. Will, as ever, was the central generator of this confident mood.

On stage their confidence was vindicated: they delivered a tight and attention-grabbing performance, on the strength of which each of the three labels invited the band to their offices for discussions. Will's masterplan had paid off. He explained that plan many years later, during an interview with the *Financial Times*. In short, it involved playing lots of concerts at colleges. 'Our theory was: let's own California,' he said. 'Let's play Berkeley, let's play Stanford, let's play UCLA, let's play USC. Let's play all the colleges so every single college kid knows us and let's create that buzz. And then we got a [record] deal.'

During those meetings, it was Will's caution and self-belief that dictated the energy. Although he and the rest of the band had dreamed for as long as they could remember of getting a full-on record contract, and although as a unit they had worked hard for over two years to get one, he was resolute that he would not shake hands on anything but the right deal. They drove to the meetings in Will's trusty VW Golf, and entered each meeting room emitting as much confidence as they could muster.

Their first meeting was with Warner Bros., and though the executive they met spoke a good game over how big his label could make the band, each band member had their doubts that he would deliver the sort of experience they were after. The next meeting, with Sony 550, did tempt them. The label was a division of Epic Records, which, as the band knew only too well, was the home of their hero, Michael Jackson. It was also the label for Des'ree and Celine Dion among many others. They listened very carefully to what the representative told them, the label's existing roster of stars meant it started with obvious advantages. The Sony executive offered them very tempting terms and promised, specifically, that she would arrange for them to appear on Oprah Winfrey's television show. It was a meeting that gave them plenty to think about ... but it would be the third and final meeting of the week that landed the contract.

Interscope impressed the band from the moment they pulled up outside its large, grand offices. They took in the framed portraits of the label's impressive roster of musicians, and sat down opposite Jimmy Iovine. His pitch to them was a winner, stating that, yes, he would make them lots of money, but that he would do so by creating something real and powerful that they were proud of. He finished his thundering pitch with the promise, 'I will blow you up into a monster group'.

Somehow, Will kept a lid on how impressed he was with Iovine's words. As Iovine anxiously awaited some response from the band, Will held off speaking for as long as he could. He asked whether the label would financially support what he and the band wanted to do more than anything at that stage: tour. With Iovine agreeing to 'throw that in as well', a deal was agreed. The advance given to the band was around half a million dollars. Once the various expenses and commissions had been paid, this left Will and each of his bandmates with around $75,000 each.

After the meeting, Will celebrated in reasonably modest style with a dinner of chicken, vegetables and rice. He was quite happy to not go crazy because, for him, to secure a record deal was just the start of a bright new future.

The immediate future was to follow just the path they wanted it to: recording and mixing in the studio during the day, and performing live in the evening. During the recording sessions the band radiated energy and endeavour. While Will was perhaps the most focused member of the band, this did not mean he took himself seriously. The studio echoed with almost as much laughter as it did music, and it was Will who generated most of that laughter and proved to be quite the clown. He would crack jokes, say silly things and pull ridiculous faces. Whatever it took to keep people amused and their spirits high, Will was there to do it. His motivational tactics worked: more and more songs were being written and recorded in these sessions, and slowly an album was coming together. It would be called *Behind the Front*, a title intended to reflect the band's yearning for authenticity. They felt that the music scene, and the hip-hop scene particularly, was dominated by people putting up a front that did not reflect their reality.

The album, released in June 1998, reflected the original songs that came from the studio sessions, together with refreshed takes on tracks that had been written for the unreleased album *Grass Roots*. As such, it embraced a lengthy period of energy, creativity and endeavour. The earliest reviews were in 'underground' publications. *Elixir* called the album 'absolutely stunning', and *Request* praised its 'incisive social commentary'. Then, sensing a bandwagon starting up, mainstream journals also asked their critics to give the record a spin. *Rolling Stone* said the album was 'an organic mixture of sampled melodies and live instruments aimed at those of us seeking a little enlightenment with our well-oiled boogie'; men's magazine *Arena* said it 'sounds great', while British weekly *Melody Maker* said it 'transcends all genres but sells out none'.

Despite these widespread and glowing reports from the critics, the album did not trouble the upper reaches of any mainstream charts, reaching no higher than number 129 in the *Billboard* charts. Likewise, their first three singles were, commercially speaking, flops. Will could later reflect on the irony in the fact that, as the band's commercial fortunes soared with future works, their stock among most of the critics would correspondingly plunge. However, for now, he was terribly disappointed by their performance. 'We haven't even gone gold, this is not a good look,' he said. Iovine told them to be patient and keep their belief. Will heeded these words but nothing could dispel his displeasure and bewilderment. Of all the band, he probably took the news hardest. After all, Will had never been of the mind that success equalled a compromise of one's principles. 'If we sell well, that's cool because we're doing something good,' he told the *Fredricksburg Free-Lance Star*. 'We can't sell out if we're doing something we enjoy. I think people miss the meaning of what selling out means.'

*

Meanwhile, in the run-up to the album's release, the band had continued to be busy on the live circuit, building awareness through more live performances. The evenings also served as introductions to a galaxy of future stars, including Eminem, Macy Gray – and Stacy Ferguson, aka Fergie.

As they adjusted to life as a fully signed band, they also shot their first official promotional video. It was a day of some excitement when the video, shot in various Los

Angeles locations, was first aired on television. The band were strolling deeper and deeper into mainstream music and enjoying every moment. It was almost like a rebirth: as Taboo put it, they were like 'ninjas pushing up street drain covers and rising into the big, wide world'.

As ninja Will stretched his limbs and regarded the big, wide world in front of him, he saw a planet replete with opportunity. Throughout his life Will has rarely missed a chance to grab an opportunity. For instance, when the Black Eyed Peas were invited on the Smokin' Grooves tour – a mobile music festival featuring several of hip-hop's biggest acts – he eschewed much of the inevitable partying that took place between performances. Instead, he networked relentlessly. The tour was peopled by countless performers who he felt could improve his band's career, starting with their next album. He took as many telephone numbers as he could from the movers and shakers.

During performances from other acts, he used his relative anonymity to eavesdrop on the feedback from audience members, stealthily mingling with the masses and noting down what they liked and disliked. This tendency of Will's helped to earn his band a nickname on the tour – the Good Samaritans. Another factor in the moniker was that the band rarely indulged in any sexual shenanigans with the plentiful beautiful females around the tour. In truth, this was less about abstinence and more due to the fact that, as the least famous act on a bill so prestigious it included Public Enemy, Busta Rhymes, Wyclef Jean and many others, the Black Eyed Peas members had to concede that they were far down the pecking order when it came to groupies and other beauties.

Will mostly enjoyed the touring experience, though he found the proximity to so many other artists a touch wearing after a while. Band vocalist at the time, Kim Hill, had a dog called Chompa, who was not a creature that Will felt any love towards, regularly shoving it off the seats on the tour bus and also occasionally growling at it, in the hope of intimidating the dog out of his personal sphere. He also had a bizarre and ultimately frustrating conversation with Public Enemy's ostentatious star Flavor Flav. Will wanted to have a deep conversation with Flav about astrology. He got a hint of the scale of the challenge ahead when, on enquiring which star sign Flav was, he received the reply: 'I am a *tarantula* ...'

A more personally rewarding experience came on the day that Will first saw one of his songs used in a film. The movie *Bulworth* had included 'Joints & Jam' in its soundtrack. The film turned out to be a forgettable and not overly successful affair. That meant little, though, as Will sat in a cinema and watched the film, his mouth spreading into a wide grin as his song came out of the big speakers. His American dream was slowly coming true.

Later, the band was invited to take part on another multi-band tour, but this time it was on a bill dominated not by hip-hop and soul artists, but *punk* acts. The Black Eyed Peas were an improbable fit for the Vans Warped Tour, but they agreed to join. Sure enough, it took them a while to win over audiences. At one show they were racially abused by some skinheads in the crowd. The angry skinheads called the band 'niggers', and told them they should 'go back to Africa'. Elsewhere on the tour, bottles were thrown and obscene hand gestures were offered by many audience members. However, the band stuck to their guns and often managed to win audiences over by the end of their set. It was often their song 'Head Bobs' that began to turn the mood. By the time they left the stage each night, they would have won some of the fans over, but as often as not it had been a tough experience. With the tour complete, the band's stature in America had grown. Now, it was time for them to fly further afield to promote their music.

Will's love affair with London, and with England in general, was about to blossom.

3 Technology and Fate

Ever since the band name-checked London during their early song 'Joints & Jam', it had seemed inevitable that they would enjoy life in the English capital. So, when they arrived in the country in September 1998, they were full of excitement. They did all the cheesy tourist things, visiting landmarks and museums, and whooping with excitement as they saw the red telephone boxes, British policemen and so on. They took walks in Regent's Park, a stunning experience as autumn was just setting in, with all the beauty that entails.

They played two nights at Camden Town's famous Jazz Café and were thrilled by the acclaim they received from the audiences in the crowded venue on Parkway, one of the district's hippest streets. London was proving to be a special place for them. Apl even commented that he felt like 'one of the fucking Beatles out there'. With UK radio stations playing their music, crowds cheering them in Camden, and the band's merchandising arm doing a healthy trade, London felt very much like a second home to Will. It was in the English capital that he rebuilt his confidence, following the disappointment of the debut album.

Back home in LA, they began work on the follow-up album in the autumn of 1999. With Will at the centre of everything, the band spent four months recording the album that would be called *Bridging the Gap*. Most of the work took place at Paramount Studios, with around fifty songs they had written, mostly on the road, since they had wrapped work on their debut. During the recording, the evidence of Will's successful networking on the road was clear for all to see. A succession of big-name artists collaborated, some of them longer-term friends or contacts of Will, but many of them names he had signed up during the Smokin' Grooves tour.

Among the names to collaborate were De La Soul, Wyclef Jean, Macy Gray, Mos Def and DJ Premier. The last also worked on the production of the overall album. Some of the 'collaborations' were actually performed remotely, with the external act sending their contribution electronically to the main studio. However, Will did work in shoulder-to-shoulder proximity to DJ Premier. The day he and his bandmates stepped into his legendary D&D Studios in

Manhattan was a proud and electrifying one for all the visitors. As far as they were concerned, they were standing in one of music's most hallowed environments, alongside their genre's finest producer.

Not everyone they approached to be involved with the album consented. For instance, Paul McCartney refused to allow them to sample the Beatles track, 'Baby You're a Rich Man'. While some critics would snipe that, in signing up De La Soul and other acts as collaborators, the Black Eyed Peas were merely trying to hang on to the coattails of bigger names, the variety of sounds and rich influences that came with them was what mattered to most listeners to the final product. Once the band had selected the final cut of tracks for the album, it was ready for release in the autumn of 2000.

Technology and fate, though, would intervene in the run-up to the September release, when several tracks from the album were leaked online. While at the time this was a frustrating development for the band, and an almost devastating one in terms of sales, it would prompt Will, in particular, to grasp the opportunities that the Internet and other technological developments offered.

The rude awakening began when, several months ahead of the album's release, Will suddenly heard some of the tracks being played by a DJ at a party. Around the same time, Will's friend Dante Santiago also heard a track being played – at a shoe store in downtown Los Angeles. When the band investigated how this could have happened, they were pointed towards the online music-sharing site, Napster. There, they found that the entire album had been leaked and was being shared for free by members. At this stage, the sharing of music online was in its infancy. Many acts were finding themselves caught out in this way.

A crisis meeting was called at the band's headquarters in Los Angeles. They huddled round a conference-call telephone connected to the record-label management. In his book, Taboo noted that Will was the most shaken up by the development. '[He] was really bent out of shape because we were not in control of our music, and he, more than any of us, hates being out of control.' The band's suspicion that they were, for now at least, essentially powerless in the face of the Napster phenomenon, hit them hard. Will, though, became consumed by an urge to grasp all the opportunities that were available in the blossoming world of technology. Within years, he would be on top of the world of the Internet. By the time he became a judge on the UK television show *The Voice*, he would be so synonymous with the Internet that his tweeting would become a topic of national debate.

More immediately, though, the actual release of *Bridging the Gap* became surrounded by disappointment. When work on the album had been completed, Will was convinced they had something very special on their hands. There would be no grand unveiling, though, merely a commercial confirmation of a release that had already taken place. Far from exceeding the disappointing sales of *Behind the Front, Bridging the Gap* actually sold less. Still, the album received a glowing tribute from *Rolling Stone*'s reviewer, who commented that whereas *Behind the Front* 'was a little too slickly produced', *Bridging the Gap* is 'a more organic-feeling representation of their considerable skills and vision. Uncluttered but muscular production, deft samples and smart rhymes all ensure that the album's power increases with repeated listenings.'

Furthermore, *Bridging* reached higher in the charts than its predecessor, peaking at number sixty-seven in America. That could not lift the mood, though, as the album sold only 250,000 copies initially. Given that it had been downloaded illegally nearly four million times, one can see the impact that the Napster leak had on the album's commercial performance. True, not all of those downloaders would have paid money for the album had that been the only way of obtaining it, but a significant proportion surely would have.

Vocalist Kim Hill, though, believes the low sales figures were unrelated to the leak. 'I doubt, very strongly, that the record sales were jeopardized by Napster,' she said. She added that the problem was the band's image: 'Three boys with sneakers and argyle socks, and a girl that actually had clothes on'. Whatever the case, the Napster leak had shaken Will. In the future, iTunes and other legitimate websites would make online music purchasing a less 'Wild West' affair, but that was no comfort at the time. To make matters worse, this would not be the last that Will and his band would hear from online leakage.

*

Will, who had dreamed of such success and worked so hard with clear ambitions in mind, was not complaining about the sudden upturn in their fortunes. While celebrating their success, he set to work thinking about how to build on it in the future. Part of that future would be further forays into solo territory. He had released his first full-length solo album, *Lost Change*, in November 2001. Due to various factors, including the 11 September attacks and – as we shall see – the rising focus on the Black Eyed Peas, the album failed to make a huge impact on the public psyche. Instead, it rather got lost, and many admirers of Will's music were not at first even aware of its existence. However, it makes for a rich and enjoyable experience that, with the benefit of hindsight, gave signposts to Will's future.

In one of the few reviews, the website AllMusic described it as: 'A sophisticated and musically enthralling endeavour that still manages to be accessible', concluding that '*Lost Change* does an admirable job of implementing a host of different styles, without losing the listener in the process.'

In contrast to his hugely commercial approach to Black Eyed Peas releases, Will was genuinely unfazed by the poor sales of his solo debut. 'It wasn't really supposed to [sell a lot],' he told *Rime* magazine. Instead, he added, he wanted it to make an impact on a handful of influential music industry figures. 'The only people I really cared about listening to it and liking it was the Okayplayer community and the Breakestra community. That's not really a lotta people – it's just tastemakers, people that care about music integrity. That's pretty much all I cared about. I got the video played on MTV – shot the video, paid for it myself, and I took it to MTV's offices and they added it. That was kinda surprising cuz it wasn't like it was [selling] mad units, and there were a whole bunch of other groups that they weren't playing.' Billing it as a 'soundtrack', Will was pleased with the outcome of his debut solo venture.

The band's next album began to be developed in November 2001 and was released two years to the month later. The heart of the album was the track 'Where is the Love?' – the song that would propel the band to dizzy new heights of fame, and was inspired by a historic tragedy. On 11 September 2001, the Black Eyed Peas were in northern California, where they had been working on new material. Will was up early and was watching television when he heard the news of the terrorist attacks on the east coast of America. He watched as the aftermath of the attacks on New York began to unfold, then rushed upstairs to wake Taboo and tell him the news. 'Shit, man, this is scary: we're being attacked!' he told his bandmate. As Taboo struggled to absorb the news, Will added: 'America is being attacked. It's the end of the fucking world, brother!'

They switched the bedroom television on and were greeted by the day's horribly iconic scene: the burning Twin Towers of the World Trade Center. 'I saw the second one hit ... right into the building,' Will told Taboo. 'Boom! I tell you, dude ... this is it! We're being fucked. We're fucked!'

As they watched the towers fall, Will's fear soared. 'We've got to go home,' he told the band, 'we've got to go home'. With all air traffic grounded in America, flying home was not to be an option for several days. Therefore, they hired wagons and a U-Haul to take them and their equipment back to New York. During the six-hour journey they sat speechless as they listened to the radio report and discuss the day's events. With a tour due to start in just forty-eight hours, the band members were not in the mood to perform

– and suspected that their audiences would not be in the mood for concerts. Yet they were also mindful that to cancel or postpone the dates would be, to an extent, allowing the terrorists who had attacked America another victory.

Will visited his grandmother to ask her advice on how they should proceed. She told him that if God had not intended their music to help heal people, then the tour would never have been arranged. She told Will that he had to offer therapy for people at the time of national crisis. 'Your music matters, and you are one of God's angels,' she said. By this stage, she scarcely needed to deliver her final verdict: that they should do the tour, as planned.

The tour itself proved to be a dramatic rollercoaster experience. Due to the involvement of Coca-Cola in the promotion of the dates, the audience size varied spectacularly from venue to venue. On occasion, this made for some peculiar experiences. In New Jersey, for instance, just thirteen fans turned up to the sizeable venue. This meant the entire audience was in the front row. Naturally, Will managed to make light of the situation by acting as if he were playing to an enormous venue, packed to the rafters. 'How y'all doin'?' he bellowed to the thirteen fans. His humour, and indeed his humility, was the saviour of the evening. The band handed pieces of fruit to each of the audience members and asked them their names so that Will could embark on improvised, personalized raps for each of them in turn.

A few nights later, in Manhattan, the audience was 400-strong. At all the dates, Will made an announcement that no terrorist could stop the world from turning or music from being made. His defiant and uplifting speeches were just what the country needed as it healed itself. Even Will's positivity was tested, though, by the atmosphere of paranoia, distrust and racism that he detected among some Americans in the aftermath of the attacks. Where, he wondered, is the love?

That question became the centrepiece of the next song they wrote. As they worked in the studio, each of the band members was trying to express how they felt about the attacks and their consequences. It was Will who came up with the idea of a child asking his mother what was wrong with the world, the conceit that became the opening lyric of the song. As the song came together, it still seemed to lack one thing: a really powerful hook to up the emotional stakes. It was Taboo who solved this vacuum, but he had to work hard to convince Will his idea was a winner.

Taboo spoke to *NSYNC pin-up Justin Timberlake, who was planning to launch a solo career, and played him the song as it stood. His task to Timberlake was to come up with a 'Marvin Gaye-style' chorus to complete the song. Within an hour, Timberlake had done so. However, when Taboo excitedly phoned Will to tell him the news, Will was less than excited. At first, he – inaccurately – dismissed Timberlake as 'the dude from Backstreet Boys'. Taboo convinced Will to hear him out and, two weeks later, Timberlake joined the band in the studio. The session got off on a bad footing, due to the fact that Timberlake had just split from his famous girlfriend, Britney Spears. At first, he was more interested in speaking about his heartache than performing the chorus he had written. The band found themselves having to act as counsellors, rather than musicians, in order to ease Timberlake back into a more positive, and, therefore, creative, frame of mind. When he finally entered the booth to sing, he quickly dispelled Will's fears. After he had sung his part, Will grinned in appreciation and told the proud Taboo that Timberlake's performance was 'dope!'.

In an interview with *Faze* magazine later, Will recalled his initial concerns about Timberlake's inclusion. 'At the time, nobody was checking for Justin,' he said. 'He had *NSYNC written all over his face. He was not cool in the urban world, not hip, not creative, not groundbreaking. I was like, why are we going to put Justin on "Where is the Love?". You put Justin on it, you're going to mess it up!'

They worked on further tracks and eventually came to the decision that they needed a female voice added to the track 'Shut Up'. The names of various candidates were discussed, including Pussycat Doll Nicole Scherzinger. In the end, they called singer Stacey Ferguson – also known as Fergie – to the studio to audition for the song. Fergie was, at this stage, only being considered to guest vocal on one track, as she had her heart set on a solo career, the launch of which she hoped Will would assist her in.

However, when producer Jimmy Iovine heard the track he not only considered it the stand-out song of the album – superior even to band favourite 'Where is the Love?'– but proof that Fergie should become a full-time member of the band. 'You need to put that girl in the group,' said Iovine. Will and his male bandmates were not immediately convinced. They decided to throw her in at the deep end by inviting her to join them onstage at a festival in Australia. Though they did not make this explicit to her, the simple truth was this: how she fared onstage would determine whether she would be invited to join the band or not.

As it turned out, Fergie slotted perfectly into their live unit and proved to have bags of charisma. Everyone agreed that she should be invited to join the band full-time. Despite her previous protestations that she was only interested in becoming a solo performer, she accepted the invitation with relish. It was a big moment for her. She had enjoyed roles as a child actress, a television presenter and then as the de facto lead singer of a three-piece girl band called Wild Orchid – and she had developed a reputation as a wild one along the way, confessing to drug addiction and lesbian experiences.

In the future, her relationship with Will would be a stormy one. For now, though, she was warmly welcomed into the band's line-up. Her appointment sealed the end of vocalist Kim Hill's place in the band. Hill's relationship with Will – which had begun with her considering him a 'little brother' – had declined. 'Things started to get a little tricky with Will and I,' she explained later to the Black Eyed Peas fan site, Portal Black Eyed Peas. 'It was very difficult for me to stand onstage and perform, because I felt like the chemistry had been tainted, and once your audience doesn't believe that what you projecting is organic, it's just not gonna work.'

With the line-up complete, the band changed their name from Black Eyed Peas to The Black Eyed Peas. Whatever their name, the group were about to experience a surge in their popularity and fame. That surge began in the summer of 2003, when they released the first single from *Elephunk*, 'Where is the Love?' The band had been invited to be the opening act for the joint-headline tour of Justin Timberlake and Christina Aguilera. Over those forty-five dates, the band measured the growing impact of their new single by the response of the audiences as they performed it live as the final number of their twenty-minute set. The single – which was released two weeks into the tour – was receiving growing radio airplay. Each evening, more of the audience would be singing and dancing along.

The single reached number eight in the American *Billboard* charts. In the UK it went to number one and became both the bestselling single of the year and the twenty-fifth bestselling single of the millennium to date. It also reached the summit of the charts in several countries in Europe, Latin America and Asia. Will and his bandmates would regularly recite out loud the words: 'Number one around the world', just to see how it felt to say them. Eight years of hard work were finally paying off.

With the success came an increase in their workload. They learned how it felt to be dragged out of bed before dawn, to spend the day in hectic promotional activities that only ended after midnight. Mainstream breakfast-television show commitments sat uneasily with nightclub appearances, but all the different demands had to be met. As they worked harder, their management attempted to keep their energy levels up by bringing them more and more good news. Nothing could stop personalities and tempers from fraying on occasion.

As well as fraught tempers, there were other consequences – and Will was the first to discover them. At the ceremony to celebrate twenty years of MTV at New York's Radio City Music Hall, he noted the toll that all this was having on Taboo. The evening is now most notorious for the kiss that was shared onstage between Britney Spears and Madonna. However, within Will's circles, there was a more immediate issue. Taboo, by his own later admission, drank three bottles of wine in just sixty minutes at the ceremony. He began to draw attention to himself with noisy, drunken behaviour. With the band due to perform at an after-show party, Will quickly decided that they would have to do so without Taboo. 'Just get him out of here before it gets any worse,' he ordered. Will had warned his errant bandmate about his hedonistic ways before. He followed up with a more direct comment, telling Taboo he had to 'slow it down'. It would be a while before Taboo heeded those words.

However, the ruthless promotional treadmill continued to move along. For nine intense months, Will and his band travelled around the world promoting, performing and partying. Taboo estimates that they gave 465 performances in a single year. The title and theme of their next album would be influenced by these heady days. All the hard work was paying off: *Elephunk* was becoming a hit around the world, propelling the band to new heights. It reached number three in the UK, number fourteen in America and charted respectably in many other territories. This was significant, as Will had told the band just before they started work on the album, that this was the big one, the make or break moment in their career. 'We haven't proved anything yet,' he had told them. With *Elephunk*'s sales, they had now.

The critical response to the album, though, was not quite so satisfying. America's influential *Village Voice* was characteristically grudging in its praise, describing the album as one 'in which the unbelievably dull El Lay alt-rappers fabricate the brightest actual pop album of 2003'. However, it was the paper's rating of 'A minus' that counted.

Rolling Stone said that 'cliched observations, preachy lyrics and MTV-ready posturing float atop meticulously detailed production'. *Entertainment Weekly* was sniffy, too. Its reviewer said that the album 'courts the mainstream with an almost comic ferocity, jumping on every bandwagon that's passed'. Thank goodness, then, for the Popmatters website, which crowned an admiring review with this thundering praise: 'If *Elephunk* doesn't move you, if you don't end up with a massive grin slapped across your face, if you don't heed the built-in dance demands, then check your pockets; there should be a receipt for your soul in there somewhere.' *Drowned in Sound* also beat the drum for the record, saying: 'Look on the surface, and you've got an album full of memorable songs, hooks that lodge in your mind ... but look in depth, and it's quality from the top down.'

In a sense, the sometimes harsh time that the band were experiencing at the pens of the critics was a result of their more admirable traits. The positivity of their message was one that sat ill at ease with the critics, who tend to be a breed more interested in 'cool' than happiness. Although Will's band have little in common with British stadium act Coldplay, both acts found that their attitude chimed enormously with mass, mainstream audiences precisely for the reason it did not with reviewers. For instance, take *Blender* magazine's review, which concluded of the band's happy attitude: 'Problem is, that kind of constant high gets as dull as life on Prozac.'

For Will, the prospect of reining in their upbeat message in order to please a handful of journalists was never on the cards. In time, more and more journalists would come to appreciate his ways, particularly those on more considered titles. For instance, when they performed at the Grammys, the *Washington Post* said theirs was 'the most impassioned performance of the night'. Their appeal to the mainstream was reaffirmed when the NBA chose the *Elephunk* track 'Let's Get Retarded' as the anthem for the play-off matches. The lyrics and title of the song were edited to 'Let's Get It

Started'. They also gave the song to the Democrat party to use for the election campaign of White House hopeful John Kerry. Will hoped the song would help send Kerry to victory over the much-maligned George W. Bush. It did not do so, but Will enjoyed his brush with politics. Next time he got involved with a presidential campaign it would be in a much higher-profile sense. An ultimately triumphant one, too.

Mulling over the critical response to their latest release, Will, in part, did understand the perspectives of the critics. 'If I was a journalist and I knew The Black Eyed Peas when they first came out and where they are now, I would write some of the same things too,' he told *The Times*. 'The way things were marketed didn't honour how it was built. But we weren't trying to make hits when we made *Elephunk*. You think I would have called the CIA terrorists [as he did in 'Where is the Love?'] right around the time America went to Iraq if I was trying to make a record to get played on the radio?'

Meanwhile, he wondered whether the post-September 11 era might herald changes in the hip-hop industry. 'Everything affects hip-hop,' he told *The Onion*. 'The question is, how does it affect the money that corporations are going to invest to put out different kinds of hip-hop? Hip-hop may offer negative feedback on the world's problems, but that's just the hip-hop that's being promoted now. There are hip-hop groups in different sectors and different communities that are doing positive shit, but corporations and companies don't want to spend the money on them that it would take to get them out there.'

Will hoped that the 'positive shit' might get more airtime and investment. Not that his focus on positivity and unity was blinkered. He realized that his vision was as vulnerable to cash-in and distortion as any. 'The only thing that I'm afraid of is that if we get too big, the labels are going to be like, "Get a fucking Indian guy, and a black guy, and a fucking Pakistani, and make them dance!" That's the only thing that I'm afraid of.'

A renewed wave of accusations that the band had sold out rolled in. 'All that "sell-out" stuff comes from the same people who held us close to their hearts for our first two records,' Will responded in an interview with *Faze* magazine. 'And they call it "sell-out" for what reason? Because we have a white girl in our group now? I don't think that just because one day you do a jazzy record and then you do a funk record means you sold out. It just means you like music and you're trying to dabble in every ray of colour in the music world.'

In 2002, the sell-out allegations had reached their peak when the band featured on an advertisement for the soft drink giant, Dr Pepper. For Will, their involvement in the project was a true 'eureka' moment. It was also something that he easily resolved in his own mind. 'I realized I made more money doing a thirty-second piece of music than two hours worth of music,' he said. He also insisted that the band retained control over all the creative aspects of the project. To him, this meant there was nothing wrong with their getting involved, whatever the snipers might say. 'If you are in control of the video, which we were, if you are in control of the clothes, the song, which we were ... what's not to like? And the people are getting the music for free anyway ... so who cares?' Will believes that even performing something as ostensibly authentic as a live concert puts his band at the epicentre of a storm of commercial activity – including the sponsorship of the venue, the petrol bought as a result of the thousands of fans driving to the concert and so on.

*

The second single from the album was called 'Shut Up', a catchy song about the break-up of a relationship, and the song that had brought Fergie to the party. It reached number one in fifteen countries. In 2010, funk star George Clinton took legal action against the band, claiming they had used a sample from his 1970s song '(Not Just) Knee Deep' without his permission. It was a testing moment for Will when news of the suit first reached him. (The case would be settled in 2012. Although the terms were not disclosed, in a court filing, mediator Gail Killefer said the settlement 'fully' resolved the dispute.)

So hectic had been the response to *Elephunk*, that for the band members it sometimes felt as if they had gone from relative obscurity to international acclaim overnight.

Will, meanwhile, had been hard at work on his second solo album. Entitled *Must B 21*, it is a seventeen-track release that was described by RapReviews.com as 'an exercise in hip-hop in its purest most unadulterated form, packed into a highly concentrated dose'. The same reviewer urged people to buy the album not just to enjoy its music, but also to support Will's solo career and the fortunes of the label, Barely Breaking Even, through which he was releasing the material. Lest the critic appear to be asking people to buy it on only a charitable basis, he concluded: 'It deserves to go gold, because it's that damn good.'

Will hired an impressive selection of fellow artists to appear on the album, including KRS-One, MC Lyte, Planet Asia and Phife from A Tribe Called Quest. Their contributions took the album to a higher plane than Will's debut solo effort. His track 'Go!' was featured on the Xbox computer game soundtrack for NBA Live 2005.

Will was about to take a break from the solo wing of his output: *Must B 21* ensured he did so from a position of some strength. When he returned, it would be in a more fully solo sense, with the mass of collaborating guests consigned to the past.

First, though, he had to hold on tight as his already soaring band rocketed ever higher. The Black Eyed Peas were proving to be an unstoppable force. No wonder a growing number of other famous artists were so keen to join the fun.

4 Collaboration

When Will attended the 2005 MOBO Awards in London, the highlight of the evening should have been the sight of hip-hop royalty Public Enemy landing the 'Outstanding Contribution to Black Music' gong. The genre-defining rap icons are a band that Will has often admired, but while he was delighted to see them recognized in this way, he was not about to switch his opportunistic senses off for the evening. His mind ticking away as quickly as ever, Will glanced around the venue to see which other musical figures were 'in the house' for the ceremony. Suddenly, he noticed that one of his all-time heroes was present. 'Shit,' Will exclaimed to his bandmates, 'it's James Brown!'

In an era in which the stature of 'legend' is awarded far too easily, Brown remains richly deserving of it. His influence on the musical scene, particularly black music, is immense. His charisma is also huge and his entourage on the night was far from insubstantial. Therefore, most people were far too nervous and in awe to even consider approaching Brown for a chat.

Will, though, is not like most people. He took a deep breath, marched over to Brown's table and introduced himself to the man he admires so much. He told the godfather of soul just how much he admires his music. Then he took the conversation to another level. 'One day,' Will told Brown, 'we would love to work with you.' It was an enormously audacious pitch. A successful one, too. 'All rigggght,' Brown told Will. 'We'll make it happen.'

He was good to his word, too. Just seventy-two hours later, Brown joined The Black Eyed Peas in their studio in Chiswick, west London. The band were only given an hour's notice of the arrival of Brown and his ten-strong entourage. Brown appeared, wearing a violet suit – described as 'sharp-ass' by Taboo – with a maroon shirt. With seven fellow musicians and three assistants in tow, he was every inch the superstar: in Taboo's telling, Brown was 'glowing' and 'oozing charisma.' He made the band feel like children in comparison. Brown's first words were to remind The Black Eyed Peas that he did not normally take part in collaborations. Why? 'I'm James Brown.' However, he said that 'something told me I needed to work with The Black Eyed Peas, and that's why I'm here. So let's work!'

Meanwhile, one of Brown's assistants gave the band a sharp reminder of Brown's stature, after Will had made a faux pas. 'Yo, what up, James, how you doing?' Will had asked as Brown arrived. Brown's assistant told Will in no uncertain terms that under the expected 'system' of behaviour, everyone was expected to refer to Brown only as 'Mr Brown'. He added that the surname form should be used universally during the session, so Will should only be referred to by other people as 'Mr I Am', while Fergie would become, for the duration of the session, 'Miss Ferg'. With that typically show-business system made clear, the artists went to work.

Will had created the foundations of the song he wanted Brown to work on with them. It was called 'They Don't Want Music', and he was nervous as he played the track as it stood to Brown, anxious for his approval. However, Brown did approve of the song and immediately took charge of the process. He told the assembled musicians of both camps that he would tell them what to do and it would be he, and only he, who would 'give you direction'.

The following hours proved an astonishing experience for Will, as he sat next to Brown at the mixing desk and watched his hero bark out orders. Will found it all both dizzyingly fun in its own right and enormously instructive. Brown told the musicians how to 'feel the funk' and make their performance perfect. Often, his orders to his own band of instrumentalists and vocalists were delivered via nothing more than a particular grunt sound, which Brown would emit and which they seemed to understand. Will watched it all with wonder.

When the ensemble moved upstairs for lunch, Will got to see Brown's diva behaviour in its full horrendous glory. Flunkies brushed his hair for him and even cut his food for him. All in all, Brown's visit to their studio had been one of the most astonishing experiences of Will's life in itself – and from it came a track for their new album.

Another special guest on the album was Sting, the former lead singer of the Police. The collaboration came about due to a separate project Will had been working on with Sting. With the band already considering sampling the melody from Sting's iconic 'An Englishman in New York' on one of the tracks for the album, it was eventually decided that they would invite him to sing on the track, which was called 'Union'. While James Brown had blown the band away with his charisma and star-like behaviour, Sting impressed them with the scale of his home, to which he invited Will and the band to stay while they were in the south-west of England to perform at the Glastonbury Festival.

Lake House, in Wiltshire, is indeed a breathtaking house and Will was mesmerized the moment he arrived at the

800-acre property in Salisbury. The opulent, castle-like main building houses some fourteen bedrooms and eight bathrooms. In the grounds stands a 350-year-old tree – the presence of which was said to have convinced Sting and his wife Trudie to buy the place. Will connected well with Sting and Trudie. Together they engaged in lengthy and deep conversations about spiritual matters. Sting also took the ensemble on a trip to the nearby attraction of Stonehenge.

*

The majority of the work on the new album, which was to be called *Monkey Business*, took place in London. The band had rented three properties in Chiswick, the one Will stayed in was a tall, narrow house in the corner of a cul-de-sac. He and the band loved the greenery of the neighbourhood and were amused by the ubiquity of pregnant women and mothers of newborn babies. It seemed to be an area of many different types of creativity – fertile ground indeed.

The band was focused and productive. As Fergie put it, they were creating a 'waterfall' that became 'this huge ocean that is *Monkey Business*'. During the three months they worked on the album in London, that waterfall flowed well. Inspiration seemed to be everywhere: following a visit to a bhangra club in London, they recorded the Bollywoodflavoured song 'Don't Phunk With My Heart'. They also recorded in France, Brazil and Japan.

Will found he was inspired in the strangest of settings. One day they were travelling in Japan on the 'bullet' train, which can travel up to 180 miles per hour. He was listening to a CD of surfing rock-style tunes when one of them, a track called 'Miserlou', inspired him to create a new song. He fired-up his laptop and began to work on the new song, using recording software he had installed for moments such as these. As the rest of the band sat drinking sake, Will was hard at work, his creative juices flowing at top speed as the train raced through Japan. Later, on a flight, he sat and worked further on the song. When the flight arrived in Tokyo, Will took his computer to the park and recorded the vocals. This was the sort of crazy way in which the album came together.

The title of the album had a degree of playful protest to it. Over the course of several years, the band had felt that the orders that their management and record label constantly bestowed upon them had almost relegated the band to the role of performing monkeys. In a harsh assessment of the band's place in the chain, Will would say, 'Sing, monkey, dance, monkey, get on stage, monkey!' But there was a secondary dimension to the simian stature they felt they had developed. As the band had been driven away from a venue one evening, so many fans had surrounded their vehicle that they felt that they were monkeys in a zoo, caged away from the visitors. Finally, the impish ways that the band adopted to get through the rigours of touring also felt, at times, like 'monkey business'. Thus the title of the new album was representative of the band's feelings at the time, capturing well the upsides and downsides of their growing fame. To a degree, it also signifies the long-term spirit of Will's band, who always believed that playfulness was a crucial part of the experience both publicly and behind the scenes.

Released in May 2005, *Monkey Business* made for an engrossing body of work. As well as the aforementioned Brown and Sting, it had guest appearances from other stars, including Justin Timberlake. Then, of course, there was the Fergie factor. On *Elephunk*, she had been a debuting oddity; now she was a mainstay of the band and therefore her contribution was keenly anticipated. With *Elephunk*, having been received so well both critically and commercially, the band risked the sort of critical backlash that so often hovers over bands who have enjoyed the favour of the reviewers.

The critics were harsh in some quarters. A regular theme the critics noted was that this fourth studio album signified a drop in form from the band's previous effort, *Elephunk*. PopMatters, for instance, sniffed: 'If ... you're in the market for dance music, although admittedly excellently produced, but which can't sustain any substantial intellectual investment, then *Monkey Business* should be right up your alley.' *Entertainment Weekly* was scarcely kinder, ranking the album 'a bland meringue: a succession of cotton candy raps about chicks, partying, and partying with chicks, broken up by choruses destined to evaporate outside a shindig's perimeter'. It even ranked the Brown collaboration as 'trite' and lacking 'much innovation'.

Rolling Stone, meanwhile, awarded the album three stars out of five, concluding: '*Monkey Business* is just as bright if not quite as fun as *Elephunk*'. The BBC attacked the album's lyrics, contending that their 'flimsiness ... may let the album down for traditional Black Eyed Peas fans who've been following the group since the days of 1998's *Behind the Front*'. The *Guardian* felt that 'the choruses are just as catchy as those on 2003's *Elephunk*,' but added that 'the lyrical inspiration has evaporated', before truly putting the boot in with the conclusion that: 'Only James Brown comes out of the wreckage of ideas and ideals with any dignity'.

Despite these harsh verdicts, the album was a commercial success: it has, at the time of writing, sold over eleven million copies worldwide. It reached the top of the album charts in eight countries, including Canada and France, and has gone triple platinum in the United States.

The album's first single, 'Don't Phunk With My Heart',

was also a hit in America: it reached number three on the US Hot 100, and won them a Grammy for Best Rap Performance by a Duo or Group. It was a number one in Australia, a number three in the UK and a number five in Canada. The second single from the album was 'Don't Lie', which reached number fourteen in the US Hot 100, and hit number six in both the UK and Australia.

The album's third single, however, proved to be a more contentious affair. 'My Humps', with its bawdy lyrics, hit number three in America. However, it was not to everyone's taste. John Bush of AllMusic called it 'one of the most embarrassing rap performances of the new millennium', which must have hurt Will, if he became aware of it. Readers of the Global Gathering website named it the dance track with 'the most ridiculous' lyrics of all time. *Rolling Stone* placed it at number one on its Twenty Most Annoying Songs chart. Kelefa Sanneh, writing for *The New York Times*, declared that the single is 'most likely to live in infamy', deliberately invoking a description of the Pearl Harbor disaster of World War II. While another critic damned it as 'so monumentally vacuous, slapped together and tossed-off that it truly tests the definition of "song"'.

Elsewhere, it was compared to Kelis's catchy 2003 hit single 'Milkshake'. Harsh words, yet Will himself would later dip a toe into the chorus of disapproval and distance himself from the track. 'It wasn't lyrical miracles,' he told the *Daily Record* in 2011. 'It got to the point where we didn't want to play it no more. But the beat was rocking.'

As they toured the album, Will was struck by a stampede of tangible signs of how far he had come. Thanks mainly due to the stature of the band, and partly due to the changing face of music-industry finance, the tour was bankrolled by two corporate sponsors: technology giants Verizon and motor company Honda. Not only did the band now travel first-class and stay in elite hotels, they were even each given a limited edition, specially manufactured Honda Civic car. Month after month they flew first-class from country to country, from continent to continent, playing to huge venues bursting with hysterical crowds. From Hong Kong to Honolulu, Tokyo to Tel Aviv, Santiago to Shanghai, they wowed audiences. Their road crew was now a multi-team operation. Even their road manager now had a considerable team at his command: the entire operation was benefiting from the band's success. Gwen Stefani was support act for several dates.

Perhaps the crowning evening of the *Monkey Business* tour came in Brazil. The band arrived at Ipanema Beach to headline a New Year's Eve concert. They did not expect the size of the crowd that greeted them: around one million people. Given that it was one million Brazilian people – often a naturally festive bunch – and the sense of occasion that the date brought to the party, and the audience made for a breathtaking, bopping vista. At the end of the show, which Will and the band crowned with an excitable rendition of 'Where is the Love?', the band feared being crushed by the audience, which began to descend en masse backstage. Will and the others were bundled into ambulances, whose sirens managed to clear a way to safety for the headlining stars.

Among the purely commercial work were more philanthropic moments, foreshadowing Will's subsequent march into such activity. While in South Africa, the band took some time out of their schedule to hold a creative event for children from deprived parts of Soweto. It was there that Will had used the example of one fourteen-year-old boy to show what was possible.

Another lad there, called Bongeni Moragelo, was like a mini-Will. As Moragelo rapped and danced, Taboo could not help but remember the Will he had first met in California, the Will who had so bossed those rapping competitions. The fire, hunger and sheer ability of the boy were astonishing. Will invited him to join them onstage in Johannesburg, a memorable moment for all concerned, particularly Moragelo. Will built a charitable sponsorship relationship with the boy, to ensure he made the most of his talents.

[Top] Entertaining his classmates: from a young age Will.i.am was mad about music.
[Above] The rapper aged sixteen.
[Left] With his beloved grandmother at the 50th Annual GRAMMY Awards.

[Above left] In the early days of the band: performing his signature move onstage.
[Above] Style icon: showcasing his unique appreciation for fashion.
[Below] After Fergie joined the band they went stellar.

[Above] Justin Timberlake provided vocals for 'Where Is the Love?', the first single from The Black Eyed Peas' third album *Elephunk*.
[Below] The band's sense of fun endears them to the masses.

[Below] Room for another one?

[Top] The Black Eyed Peas hit the big time with their award for Best Rap Performance at the GRAMMYs in 2005.
[Above] A hit with young fans at 2005's Teen Choice Awards.

[Above] Will.i.am uses his fame for good as he provides some much needed support for victims of natural disasters.
[Below] Performing at a tsunami benefit concert with James Brown and Justin Timberlake in 2005.

Rubbing shoulders with the rich and famous of the movie, music and fashion worlds alike.

[Left] Performing onstage in 2007 with Pussycat Doll Nicole Scherzinger, who was originally approached to join The Black Eyed Peas.
[Below] Another all-star collaboration: performing with Usher in 2010.

Tonight's gonna be a good night: Will.i.am is a born entertainer.

Also during the trip, the band met South African legend and ex-President Nelson Mandela. It was a proud day for Will, who wore a neat white suit for the occasion. He was unimpressed by Taboo's comparative shabbiness of dress and punctuality, chiding his hung-over bandmate with a sarcastic: 'Hey, glad you could join us', when his still-wayward bandmate arrived.

This was an understated rebuke to a bandmate and friend who Will loves, rather than anything rougher than that. It would be easy for Will to have descended into full-blown diva behaviour at such exciting moments as huge concerts and introductions to iconic world leaders, especially after seeing how his hero James Brown had behaved in the simple surroundings of a recording studio. Yet he has largely maintained a sense of humour and balance. His demands on the road have rarely been monstrous. They mostly centre around the space and ability to continue his songwriting and creativity wherever he is.

However, one way to have him turn his nose up is to present to him a lavatory with no moist baby wipes as an option. If there is only 'dry toilet paper', he will not be happy. To describe why this is important, he constructs a metaphor which is best skipped by the queasy or those eating. 'Here's proof on why people should have baby wipes: get some chocolate, wipe it on a wooden floor, and then try to get it up with some dry towels,' he told *Elle* magazine. 'You're going to get chocolate in the cracks. That's why you gotta get them baby wipes.' When he puts his case that way it is terribly difficult to argue.

Will was, at this stage, living in a fine home, in which the presence of baby wipes was just one of the luxuries. The $7m home, near Griffith Park in the Los Feliz neighbourhood, was physical testament to his success. Particularly poignant and significant was the fact that from the roof of his house, Will had a commanding view of the city, all the way to the building in which he grew up. Although the properties were nearly twenty miles apart, the symbolic distance was even greater. With a neat, terraced garden accompanying the lavish building, Will was living in some comfort. He had designed the house so he could work and record in almost any of its rooms – and beyond. 'It's not really a house,' he told *The Times*, 'it's a studio. There are microphones and places I can plug in everywhere; a wireless controller, so I can record from anywhere; and I can log on from anywhere in the world, so even if I'm in London or Tokyo, I can still be making music.'

Indeed, even after purchasing this property, Will continued to sleep most evenings in a hotel, even when his itinerary did not require him to. Although the hotels he chooses are plush, including one overlooking London's

Hyde Park, he is happiest with a fairly small room. 'I like to be cosy,' he said. 'I need a place to recharge.'

*

After releasing his first two solo albums in fairly quick succession, Will had taken a few years out from solo releases. In 2007, the third was finally unveiled. It was originally going to be titled *Keep the Beeper*, but the title Will eventually settled on was *Songs About Girls*. Taking at face value the widespread perception that this piece of work is at least semi-autobiographical, here we get a rare glimpse into Will's personal life. Indeed, as he explained to *Billboard*, it was the personal dimension of the project that encouraged him to persevere with it, when he could just as easily have scrapped the work and concentrated on his band. Instead, he ploughed on with the album 'where all the songs could tell a story of falling in love, falling out of love, trying to get back in love, destructing love and destroying love and then starting a new situation. That journey is what makes this unique.' *Rolling Stone* magazine described the narrative of the album as: 'Boy meets girl. Boy gets girl. Boy goes to strip club. Boy gets caught cheating. Girl leaves. Boy and girl somehow get back together.'

In an imaginative overall package for the album, Will

recorded videos for eight of the twelve songs, creating, in his words, 'a movie about making a movie'. Even more worthy of note was the online music player he developed to accompany the album. The music player, developed alongside technology company Musicane, enabled Will to add to the album's track list as many times as he wished, with the fans sharing the profit. Fans could embed the player on their own websites, blogs or MySpace pages. Then, each time a visitor downloaded a song from that player, the website owner would share in Will's profits.

'I thought, "If I have an album filled with songs about girls, what happens if tomorrow I write another song about a girl?"' he told *The Times*. 'So something that started off just with fifteen songs, in the next ten years could have 100 songs. Having twelve songs on a record? That day is done.' He described his media player arrangement for *Songs About Girls* as 'the whole multimedia enchilada'. Fans enjoyed both snacking and feasting on the music tortilla and its contents.

The album had originally been due to include collaborations with Slick Rick, Ice Cube, Q-Tip, Common, Snoop Dogg, Too Short, Busta Rhymes and Ludacris. However, the only one that made the final version was that with Snoop Dogg, who appears on 'The Donque Song'. In due course, Cheryl Cole would contribute backing vocals to the single release of one of the tracks.

The BBC reviewer felt that the lack of collaborators made the album a lesser thing, saying: 'The soulless record would have benefited from Adams tapping up contributors from his extensive list of heavyweight contacts and adding some bite to its bark'. That said, the reviewer was less than impressed by the one guest appearance that did make it, describing it as: 'Snoop Dogg's most vacuous cameo for some time'. The Sputnikmusic reviewer was even harsher on the album. 'There's not even one song here that sounds good enough to be a big single,' he wrote, declaring the record 'an abject failure on practically every level'.

Entertainment Weekly was similarly comprehensive in its dismissal of the album as a: 'half-assed exercise in superficiality', while *Slant Magazine* attacked its 'appallingly bad' lyrics. AllMusic was far more impressed, awarding the album the honour of the 'best album-length production of the year', and declaring it 'a tour de force of next-generation contemporary R&B', that 'percolates with more innovation, enthusiasm and excitement than contemporary work by Pharrell, Kanye West, Mark Ronson, or anyone else remotely in the same league'. Commercially, the album outperformed his previous solo efforts but still failed to make much of a dent in the charts. For the time being, Will's solo adventures would be relatively disastrous commercially when compared to the mammoth success his band was increasingly enjoying.

In promoting the album, Will gave glimpses into his personal life. He described to the *Guardian* how he makes relationships with women work. 'These days I'm a masseuse and a cook,' he said. 'Then I become a cuddler, and a spooner. I'm a conversationalist. I just like to talk – to have random conversations about odd things, like dance music and jogging. If you don't talk about a girl's interests, then forget it. You need to inspire them to achieve all the things they want to achieve. As well as just saying, "You look hot today". And in a good relationship, time is nothing. You've got to always keep your phone on, you've got to get Skype, get a webcam, get MSN, get Yahoo; get 'em all. You know? So you're always available. That's hot.'

As well as communication, he said, he is also keen on honesty in relationships – but only from a realistic starting point: 'And you've got to try your hardest not to lie. But you can't say you're never going to, because then you're lying.' Fine words, yet Will's personal life continued to be an enigmatic affair.

With his third solo album on the shelves, albeit not moving from them with much enthusiasm, Will turned his attention back to The Black Eyed Peas. However, he also had his fingers in a splendid feast of other pies. From production to politics, Will was spreading his gaze far and wide. First, though, he had to weather an emotional storm.

Will sets the scene of how he felt at the start of 2008. 'I was feeling depressed,' he later told the *Daily Mail*. So he decided that the best way to beat his blues was to drive out to the freeway and spray some graffiti, or 'tag', in Will's lingo. 'I stopped under a bridge on Route 101 and wrote "No" in big letters using a can of black paint,' he said. 'I'd almost finished when two cops arrived.' There then ensued a chase. Will was unsuccessful in his getaway plan and ended up adding physical pain to the emotional torment he was suffering. 'I broke out running across the freeway, tripped and broke my fifth metatarsal bone,' he said. According to the Young Hollywood website, Will's representative refused to comment on whether there had been any further repercussions after this incident.

What he really needed was not to spray graffiti, but to find something that would reignite his fire. Such an opportunity was just around the corner.

*

The election campaign that propelled Barack Obama to the White House in 2008 was one of the slickest and most innovative force fields in political history. Just as John F.

Kennedy had first harnessed the power of television during his campaigning in the 1960s, so did Obama successfully grapple with a new campaigning medium: the Internet.

At the centre of his online electioneering was the slogan 'Yes We Can', and Will directed a campaign video harnessing this slogan into a musical force. It was inspired by a speech in which the candidate moved millions of listeners – including Will himself. 'It made me reflect on the freedoms I have, going to school where I went to school, and the people that came before Obama like Martin Luther King, presidents like Abraham Lincoln that paved the way for me,' he told *ABC News*.

The video he made was imaginative and attention-grabbing. It featured Will and a few dozen other stars including Scarlett Johansson, Nicole Scherzinger, Adam Rodriguez, Amber Valetta and Nick Cannon, speaking and singing along to a video of Obama's benchmark speech. Will had teamed up with Jesse Dylan, the filmmaker son of Bob Dylan, to direct the ambitious project. Over forty-eight hours, they invited the galaxy of stars to pass through their studio and film their contributions to the campaigning collage. 'I'm blown away by how many people wanted to come and be a part of it in a short amount of time,' said Will when the project ended. 'It was all out of love and hope for change and really representing America and looking at the world.'

The video, clocking in at a little over four minutes long, is shot in basic black-and-white, and its sparse and simple feel adds to the 'community' feel of the work. However, this on-the-surface modesty belies the slickness and thoughtfulness that went into its making. It premiered on ABC News in February 2008. However, as had always been the intention, the video's true impact and influence was felt online, after it was uploaded onto the YouTube network and shared on Obama campaign websites. The online onslaught began on the campaign's 'Super Tuesday'. It became a truly viral effort and has now been watched over twenty-six million times. In August, Will performed the song live at an Obama campaign convention in Colorado, where his energetic performance whipped the crowd into quite a frenzy.

By this stage, the overall campaign was gathering such momentum that an Obama victory began to seem inevitable. Will's part in that campaign was significant: it was to a large degree thanks to this video that the 'Yes We Can' slogan became so well known worldwide. However, the video was not without its critics. A *Wall Street Journal* writer described it as 'deeply creepy', dismissing its stars as people who 'appear to be in some sort of trance', before concluding 'the whole thing has the feel of a cult of personality'. Other critics, including ostensible supporters of Obama, claimed to be 'weirded out' by it all.

None of these criticisms stood in the way of the video's momentum, however. It won an Emmy award for 'Best New Approaches in Daytime Entertainment', with the panel praising its 'passion and inspiration'. Will's fellow executive producer of the video, Fred Goldring, said: 'We are thrilled and honored to have received a prestigious Emmy Award, particularly in a brand-new category which acknowledges the ever-increasing impact of the convergence of digital content and delivery'.

In the same week as that announcement, Will was crowned 'Artist of the Year' at the Webby Awards. His acceptance speech was just five-words long: 'Now we know we can'.

So, what did Will hope an Obama victory would bring with it? Another Obama slogan was 'Change we can believe in'. As for Will, the change that he said he wanted Obama to bring to America, should he be elected, included: 'Education, America's finance, getting our dollar back to where it should be, stopping the war, health and international policies.' As his political clout increased, somewhat surreally, Will even appeared as a hologram on CNN News to discuss the election.

As a result of the frenzy of expectation that had been built around him, Barack Obama entered the White House with considerable pressure on his relatively young shoulders.

A significant number of his most vocal supporters would subsequently feel disappointment during the President's first term. Will would have some issues with President Obama, too, but his pride at having played such an influential part in the election of the President of what many still consider the planet's most powerful country was, rightly, undiminished. Will received generous thanks from Obama, who told him his video had made a significant difference to the campaign. 'The President has thanked me tons of times since,' Will said. 'He told me I reached a demographic that had been, up to that point, invisible.'

In his journey on the political carousel, Will has striven to remain sincere. Mindful of how empty and insincere are the political or social gestures of many stars, he has tried to eschew such vanity. 'If I go out and say, "Yes We Can! We can, Obama! I support Obama!" And then I'm out, going, "Woohoo, I'm not even living in America, I'm in Spain!" How is that supporting? Because I go to a freaking fundraiser and give him some money sometimes?'

Will has stated that he wishes more people would notice how little control we have over what happens in the world. 'We're not in control,' he told the *Independent*. 'We have no control over the outcome of anything. Like the planet and global warming, we don't control that. If politicians want a war, we don't control that. Acts of terrorism, we can't control them.' In another moment of cynicism, he said: 'Politics are about preserving relationships at the end of the day, and it has nothing to do with the greater good for humanity. It's just all about business.'

The final word on his association with Obama to date can only be a brief recounting of a highly embarrassing moment Will had while performing at the President's inauguration. Of all the memories of the experience that Will expected to take away with him on the day, the one he had not bargained for was that he would break wind in front of the President. 'I'd been eating all sorts of rubbish and my insides were in a mess,' he explained to the *Daily Mail*. 'I wasn't healthy like I am now. I was playing on stage and I just couldn't help myself.' The audacity of wind, indeed. Nowadays, he does indeed eat carefully and healthily, including the hellish-tasting yet supremely effective 'superfood' of kale juice. (He might not be entirely out of the woods, though, as kale is notorious for producing supremely blustery conditions down south.)

*

Meanwhile, his stature as a producer for other artists was soaring. Having taken production duties on releases from The Black Eyed Peas and his own solo ventures, Will had learned a great deal about the craft. His technical knowledge and ability, together with his mesmeric persona, combined to make him quite a prospect. Over the years, Will has worked with several of the music industry's biggest names, including some he personally has admired for several years. His talent, stature and energy have combined to make him an attractive prospect for other artists. From 2004, his name appeared on the production credits of material by a wide variety of artists, including Carlos Santana, the Pussycat Dolls, Ricky Martin and Earth, Wind & Fire. He also worked for Diddy, Nas and Justin Timberlake during these restless years.

To date, the pinnacle of such experiences came in 2006, when he was invited to work with Michael Jackson. He spent a large part of the year working with Jackson in Ireland. For Will, to work with 'the biggest inspiration' of his life, the man who 'defined me, and my dreams' was a blissful honour. It hardly felt like work at all.

This was not the first time his career had crossed paths with Jackson's, but never before had it done so on such a scale. He could have looked back to when he first walked into the offices of Epic Records in the 1990s. At that time, even to be in the same building as the label that owned Jackson's music seemed to be honour enough. So, when he was first told that Michael Jackson was on the phone, wanting to speak about their working together, Will assumed it was somebody playing a practical joke. Now, working alongside Jackson in the studio day after day, 'felt like a dream' to Will. For Jackson said he chose Will to work with because he felt he was making 'wonderful, innovative, positive, great music' and therefore was curious to see 'how the chemistry would work'.

It made for a surreal experience for Will at times: 'You're there in Ireland. It's green hills. It's Michael Jackson. You're in the cottage making beats, dance beats. He's like dancing and sh*t.' His nerves could be forgiven. Naturally, there were many such moments of eccentricity. One morning, Jackson suggested Will ride a horse out to the fields. 'Why don't you go pick some apples?' Jackson asked him. 'Take the horses, they're lovely, they're wonderful. They know exactly where the juicy apples are!'

Will took up the challenge and, for the first time in his life, got on a horse. Jackson had advised Will that if he noticed the horse trying to grab an apple that he should 'grab it before he does – because that will be the juiciest apple'. Will decided that the best policy would be to share the juicy apples with the horse: each time the horse went to grab one with its mouth, Will would let it have that one, and take a neighbouring apple himself. This seemed the best compromise with a beast that had the potential to throw him off.

Work continued on the album in surroundings that Jackson had become very fond of. He had found Ireland a haven from the media frenzy that perpetually surrounded him and he had worked at the studio in County Westmeath before. And it certainly suited Will to work with Jackson in serene surroundings.

The tracks they were working on were supposed to form a comeback album for Jackson. It was to be a dance album, full of the life that was, unbeknown to them both, soon to leave Jackson for good. The material they were working on was, said Will later, of a high standard. 'It was going to be out of this world,' he told the *Mirror*. 'It's something Michael has never done before – a dance music album. I was very proud of it.' Will noted, with somewhat amused approval, how serious Jackson was about his work. 'But he was very protective and kept it under lock and key. After we made it I had to hand back every demo. He was a perfectionist and didn't want anyone to hear it until it was ready.'

Will also noticed Jackson's perfectionism when the singer visited him at his house. There, he watched as Jackson spent three hours fine-tuning his voice, just in order to sing for five minutes. Will was impressed. 'He's laying and his feet are up on the chair, he's kicking his feet,' he said. 'I'm like, dude, Michael Jackson's laying on my floor. Michael Jackson's laying on my floor. He's testing his voice and three hours has passed.' Will was astonished but approving. Jackson told him: 'I just love, you know, this is all we have is flesh and bones. That's it. It's just flesh. That's all we got. I want to protect it and take care of it, because this is my voice. This is my thing.'

Will emerged from his association with Jackson replete with several cracking anecdotes, which he has related with aplomb. One involved some contact he had with the King of Pop while they were both staying in Las Vegas. Jackson phoned Will to let him know he was in town. Will mentioned that The Black Eyed Peas were playing a concert that evening, and invited Jackson along. Initially, Jackson was excited, but when Will told him the band's stage time was 9 p.m., Jackson said: 'Oh, rats, I can't. I've got to put the kids to sleep.' Will was charmed and amused by Jackson's use of the word 'rats'.

He issued Jackson with another invitation, telling him he was also due to appear onstage with Prince later in the evening, and asking if he would like to watch. 'Oh really? I'd love to. Call Prince and see if it's cool,' replied Jackson. Will could hardly believe what was happening, as he phoned Prince's team to ask them whether it was OK if Michael Jackson watched him perform alongside Prince. Naturally, the answer was affirmative.

He ended up running late for the performance, and

worried he might miss it all together. He could hardly believe the day he was having. 'So, I'm late, I'm late,' he told CraveOnline. 'I'm in the cab, like aw, man, what a time to be f*ckin' late. I'm always late and I'm late for Michael Jackson to see me perform with Prince. So I hop off the cab and I'm running in Las Vegas.' As he ran down the road, towards the Palms venue, people recognized him – almost. 'I'm running and people are like, "Wyclef!" I'm like, "F*ck you", right? Then I run and I get to the place and I perform for Prince and I walk off stage and Michael's there. He's like, "That was awesome!"' A proud, and bizarre, moment for sure. 'Yeah, but that was a great experience to have Mike see me perform with Prince. It was nuts. That's great, cool.'

On 25 June 2009, Michael Jackson died. Will was shocked and devastated when he learned the news while in Paris. The band had just performed and were letting their hair down at the VIP Room nightclub, a short distance from the Champs-Elysées. Will was DJing and, in a less busy moment, picked up his phone to check for messages. To his horror, one of the messages he found told him that Jackson had died. Given that there had been rumours in the past of Jackson dying, he hoped this would turn out to be another hoax. Sadly, after checking with Quincy Jones, he discovered that this time the superstar really had passed away.

At this stage, Will could have lived by the motto of 'the show must go on'. Instead, he brought the 'show' to a crashing conclusion. He cut dead the music and announced over the microphone the news he had just had confirmed to him. The festive atmosphere disappeared in an instant, and tears were shed – some of them from Will's eyes.

Will had spoken to Jackson just four days before, he later revealed. 'He called me to wish me happy Father's Day even though I don't have any children. He said, "I just wanted to call and say have a good day anyway." I told him, "OK, I will grab my crotch and wish myself happy Father's Day for all my unborn children." He laughed and said, "You're so funny."'

In fact, Jackson's gesture touched Will deeply. He realized that, for fatherless Will, Father's Day could be an emotional challenge. The call was Jackson's thoughtful way of reaching out. Will had attempted to contact him around the same time, but found that Jackson was forever busy. His last contact, albeit indirectly, with Jackson had been just days before his death, when, while Will was DJing at a club in Wandsworth, south-west London, one of Jackson's choreographers approached him. 'He came over and told me Michael wanted to get the Peas to open his gigs at the O2,' said Will in *Billboard* magazine. 'Man, that would have been so amazing. Imagine us together on stage. Awesome.'

Instead, fate intervened. 'It's so sad,' said Will, reflecting on Jackson's death. 'He was my friend and the biggest inspiration of my life. I'm going to miss him.'

Before long, he felt he had to go to war on behalf of his friend and inspiration. In 2010, a posthumous album of Jackson tracks was released. Will was utterly horrified. He first spoke out in August, as publicity for the album, *Michael*, began. 'How you gonna release Michael Jackson when Michael Jackson ain't here to bless it?' he asked, rhetorically, in the *NME*. After the album's producer said that he was following Jackson's 'notes and plans', the row rolled on.

Several parties made conflicting claims to understand and be serving Jackson's wishes. The man himself was unable to clear matters up, so Will did his best to honour his friend's wishes. As part of this process, he related a conversation the two had about a leaked song. 'A couple of months before Michael died he called me on the phone really upset,' he said. '[Jackson said] "Hey, it's Michael, somebody leaked one of these songs." And I said, "What song, Mike?" And he said, "Some song called 'Hold My Hand'." I swear to God, I had this conversation with him.' Having been hit by leaked tracks himself, Will could empathize with Jackson's feelings.

As for *Michael*, Will was forthright in his assessment of

its release. 'Whoever put it out and is profiting off of it, I want to see how cold they are,' he told the Sun. 'To say that what [Jackson] contributed during his life wasn't enough. He just wasn't any ordinary artist. He was a hands-on person. To me it's disrespectful. Michael Jackson songs are finished when Michael says they're finished.' Akon, the artist who collaborated with Jackson on the song that became the posthumous single 'Hold My Hand', hit back, saying: 'I think that's probably Will's opinion. Me personally, I think that's keeping his legacy alive. I don't see anything disrespectful about it. He got his people taking care of it. We all did records that we actually worked on together on the album. These records would have come out whether he was alive or dead, so I think this actually helps to keep his legacy alive. I honestly disagree with that.'

Will remained robust in his position, saying he would only change his mind about posthumous releases if Jackson's mother were to contact him and say the plans had her blessing. Until such a point, any releases of unfinished Jackson material would only be made, said Will, by 'freaking parasites!'.

Putting the tragedy of Jackson's death and the subsequent controversy to one side, it had been an immense experience for Will to work with him. Nothing could change that. So much more could have come of their working relationship, had Jackson not died. Will says he was on the brink of setting up a duet between Jackson and Cheryl Cole. 'I told Michael Cheryl was the hottest thing in the UK and he was keen to meet her,' he told the *People*. 'I was gonna write them a song.'

For Will, Jackson will never be bettered commercially. 'He holds the highest amount of records that you could sell – no one's ever going to sell that amount of records,' he said. 'Why? Because there are no more record stores. So you're never going to beat his records. Never, ever, ever in the history of records in life.' His deep respect for Jackson partially explains why Will refused to accept any expenses from Jackson for the time he spent working with him in the studio. The remainder of the explanation is that Will had grown appalled by the tales of 'hangers-on' taking advantage of Jackson and his wealth.

'A week before the trip, he was like, "My manager is gonna call you to make sure all the travel stuff [is taken care of]",' Will told Starpulse. '[He asked me] "Do you fly commercial or private?" I was like, "Don't worry about my flights; I'll pay for my flights ... So many people have taken advantage of you in the past ... it will be my honour to take myself there and let's just make music to make music. You don't pay for my flight, I won't charge you my fees and if we make good music then the song will make [me] money."

He's had a history of people just taking advantage of his success and camping out in the studio and charging him outrageous rates.'

The exploitation continues to this day: in March 2012, Jackson's entire back catalogue, including the tracks he collaborated on with Will, were stolen from Sony by online hackers. It was a posthumous reminder of the sort of trends that Jackson had talked to Will about when, remembered Will, Jackson told him 'how cruel people can be'. Will has also spoken of how cruel he felt the media was to Jackson. While Will has never made a clear statement on his feelings over the sexual-abuse allegations that haunted Jackson, he has spoken of the unfair level of 'scrutiny' his friend and idol had to face during his life.

One is left with a sense of lost opportunity. Jackson came across as an increasingly spent force in the latter years of his life. Both creatively and personally he seemed to be in the depths of the doldrums. Yet there was no doubting his talent and potential. A key element he lacked in his life was the presence of a sincere, gifted and enthusiastic backer. He did get one, in the form of Will, but sadly it was too late. One can only speculate as to what the two men could have created together had there been more time.

'Something needs to put a jolt back in the music industry,' said Will, interviewed in *Access Hollywood* alongside

Jackson in 2006. 'The only person that can put that jolt back in it, that monstrosity of entertainment and music is the one that created it.' By that, he meant Jackson. During the same interview, Jackson was asked whether he wanted his comeback to be a gradual, tentative affair, or something bigger than that. The King of Pop seemed uncertain how to answer, his lack of confidence clearly on show. 'I can answer that as a fan,' said Will, intervening. 'Big'. In retrospective it's a chilling moment, underlining what Will could have offered the wayward superstar.

How to sum up what an icon Jackson had been to Will? In an emotional video blog in 2012, he put into context what Jackson had meant to him, as he grew up. 'When you're in the ghetto surrounded by crime and violence,' said Will his eyes welling up as he searched for the right words. 'You gave me escape. I escaped from all the drama around me, listening to your music. Thank you, Michael Jackson. Thank you for your dedication, thank you for your music, thank you for the dreams. I used to wanna dance like you. I used to draw pictures of you.' Describing Jackson as 'the king of the industry', he declared that 'there will never be another artist who will impact the industry the way you have'.

Will has, though, worked with other musical icons, including pop princess Britney Spears, on her seventh album, *Femme Fatale*. 'I just came from the studio right now,' he told Associated Press, following one of their sessions. 'It's a monster. It's mean, pretty, edgy, next level. But the beat just ... It's that beat. She's singing fresh over it. It's something that today needs.'

In a separate interview, with *Extra*, he elaborated. 'It's mean, but a nice mean. It's hard, but melodic. It's aggressive, but smooth. It's the next level, but today. She's a sweetheart. We made music and that's what I like. When you're doing things because you just love it, without the, ya know, "we need a single" pressure, when you're just in there having fun, that's what I love.'

His boyish enthusiasm shines through afresh in his words. One senses that, to a large extent, it is when producing for other artists that Will is at his happiest. The innocence he feels in such scenarios is robbed from him when working with his own band, with all the added pressure that entails.

He has also entered that bubble of innocence with Irish rock icons U2. He felt too nervous and in awe of them to suggest one of his songs for them to record. Instead, he said, he stuck to production duties. 'I recorded for a month with U2. Even though I worked with Michael Jackson, their U2-ness intimidated me,' he told *NME* magazine. Indeed, Will has been accused of borrowing the melody for 'I Gotta Feeling' from the U2 track 'I'll Go Crazy If I Don't Go Crazy Tonight'.

Jimmy Iovine has pointed out that there is a connection between the tracks, but only in the sense of inspiration. 'I sent will.i.am over to the studio to do some remixes on "I'll Go Crazy",' he told the *Sun*. 'He works on them for two weeks, comes back and writes "I Gotta Feeling".' Iovine added: 'The chords are U2 chords, 100 per cent. Will even told them.'

Will's excitement at working with rock gods U2 might surprise some. However, his musical tastes are far broader than casual perusal might suggest. Furthermore, Will was inspired by the band's longevity as much as anything. Formed in 1976, the Irish band has dominated the music scene since they first enjoyed chart success in the mid-1980s. 'I look at U2 and think, "Wow, I hope our group can stay together that long and still make brilliant music",' Will told the *Sun*. 'And just being around Bono and the guys is inspiring. It's like how a government should be. Bono for president of the world, I say.'

When The Black Eyed Peas had toured with U2, they had been impressed by how down to earth the Irish front man was. In sharp contrast with their experience with the Rolling Stones a few years earlier, the two bands had mingled happily backstage. In his autobiography, Taboo writes that the most contact they had was a brief 'Hi, guys', from the Stones, before going their separate ways. There were no hard feelings from Will and his band over this – Will would later work with Mick Jagger – but the open and friendly Bono certainly made a refreshing change.

It is little wonder that Will so admires the energetic Bono: the tireless way in which Will himself approaches life is remarkable. Observed from afar it would be hard to believe that here was a man already a multimillionaire. Although the royalties from his Black Eyed Peas material were rolling in, he continued to work with the ferocity and energy of a man struggling to keep his financial head above water. No amount of money, it seemed, could satisfy his hunger, not least because Will has never been motivated by purely financial dreams. Rather, it is the satisfaction of creativity and positivity that so drive him.

His fortune was about to be added to dramatically, though, as the band released a song that would dwarf even the iconic 'Where is the Love?'.

5 The E.N.D. and the Beginning

During the summer of 2009, The Black Eyed Peas made chart history when they had singles simultaneously at number one and number two in the US *Billboard* chart. How they got to such a position itself tells the story of their fifth album: *The E.N.D.*

For Will, that story began down under in Sydney, Australia. He was there to film his part in a new movie, *X-Men Origins: Wolverine*. Having made his cinematic debut voicing the part of a hippo named Moto Moto in the 2008 animated film *Madagascar: Escape 2 Africa*, he took a step up with the *X-Men* franchise. He explained his role, and its filming, in an interview with MTV. 'I'm a teleporter, I'm here, I'm there, I'm everywhere. Boom, boom, boom!' he said. 'My character's name is John Wraith. He's a black Texan. He's not a cowboy, but his gear suggests that he is. He's just a badass who'll whoop your ass.'

He was so excited to land the part, and had a battle scar

to show for his involvement. He explained that he acquired the scar during the filming of an intense scene. 'It was my fight scene. I was real into it, and then I missed my mark, and I punched the camera and broke the lens! But that goes to show you. I ain't to be messed with, because I break lenses!'

The camera was fixed and filming resumed, but, by Will's own admission, the scene had to be reshot a number of times before he nailed it. 'It probably took me fifty times, but I got it. It was hard for me, but it was cool and fun at the same time.' (Another challenge the experience threw up was its placing of Will alongside the action-movie hero actor Hugh Jackman. Will said that this made him feel fat in comparison. 'Hugh is ripped, man,' he told the *Daily Mail*. 'I saw him every morning and felt bad about my body.')

While filming in Australia, he had asked some youngsters where the best hip-hop clubs could be found. They could not know it at the time, but their reply would ultimately shape the sound of the next Black Eyed Peas' album. They told him that as far as they were concerned it was not hip-hop that was cool any more, but electro music. He investigated the scene and was enlivened and inspired as a result. He loved this new sub-genre of dance music, with its basic, but almost hypnotizing, beats.

He returned to Los Angeles even more inspired than

usual and told his bandmates all about his discovery. Together, they continued and deepened the research into the burgeoning electro scene so they could incorporate it into their own material.

Taboo was not immediately won over by the plan, but Will was insistent. 'This is the shit that is going to take us to places we have never been,' Will told him. He then told the rest of the band that the electro sound was going to do 'big things', so it was imperative that they all 'listen to it, learn it, study it, believe it – and become it'. It was the most excited he had been for some time, and his bandmates took heed of his words. They had lost count of the number of times that Will's policy announcements had proved winners.

The result of their immersion in electro was their fifth album, *The E.N.D.* The title has two meanings. First, it was the band's subtle and mischievous dig at the media, which had for some years been predicting the band would split – even at one point reporting that it had. To Will's surprise, the media seemed unable or unwilling to compute the concept that he could have a solo career at the same time as being fully committed to his band. To them, his solo activity could only mean he was about to jump ship.

He thought the title he chose for the album might 'cause some controversy'. The initials of the title stood for 'Energy Never Dies', a clever inversion of the word they spelled out. They worked on the album in London – where they returned to the Metropolis Studios – and Los Angeles. David Guetta produced the album, having had a curious introduction to Will in Ibiza. While partying in a nightclub, Will was passed a microphone and invited to perform some impromptu rap. Only later did he realize that the man who had passed him the mic was Guetta, a Frenchman who has been a leading light of the dance scene for decades. He contacted Guetta and invited him to work with the band on their new material.

These were fertile times for the band, and their sessions resulted in a long list of around fifty songs from which to choose for the final cut. Eventually, the track list was cut down to just fifteen songs, which formed *The E.N.D.*, a piece of work that Will himself described as: 'an album that was about escapism – light on grey matter but heavy on good-time vibes'.

In no other track on the album – indeed, in no other song ever released by the band – was the good-time vibe stronger than on the one that became their biggest hit, and the song that is so widely associated with them. It was Guetta who provided the spark that ignited into this monstrously successful party hit. He sent Will a basic beat, which immediately set him into action. Just over an hour later, Will had developed it into the best part of a song, which would be called 'I Gotta Feeling'. Interestingly, as Taboo reveals in his memoir, at first, the band did not realize what a hit they had on their hands. They loved the song but had no idea how huge it was to become. Will was unabashed about the song's message, and its part on the album.

'It's dedicated to all the party people out there in the world that want to go out and party,' he told *Marie Claire*. 'Mostly every song on The Black Eyed Peas record is painting a picture of our party life. It was a conscious decision to make this type of record. Times are really hard for a lot of people and you want to give them escape and you want to make them feel good about life, especially at these low points.'

Another pivotal song on the album was called 'Boom Boom Pow', in which the electro influence could be strongly heard. Heavy on beat but light on lyrics, it was an unlikely hit, but a hit all the same. It only became a single by chance, after a rough version of it was somehow leaked on the Internet. Will decided the best response to the unfortunate leak was to release the song as a single right away. Although the band had never considered it to be a radio-friendly song, they put it out as a single to see what the reaction would be. Contrary to their assessment, the song turned out to be hugely popular on the airwaves. It received, in the words of Taboo, 'humungous' airplay and sold enough copies to reach number one four weeks after its sudden release. The band was stunned that this unfancied song had reached the summit. Imagine their surprise, then, when it stayed there for the best part of three months. It was also a number one hit in Britain, Canada, Belgium and Australia.

If the band believed this was to be the peak of their success, they were about to be pleasantly surprised. When 'I Gotta Feeling' was released, on 16 June, 'Boom Boom Pow' was still enjoying itself at number one. On its release, 'I Gotta Feeling' went straight to number two, giving the band their top-two domination. At that stage, only eleven bands in US chart history had managed that feat, and it had been five years since anyone had pulled it off.

As 'I Gotta Feeling' became a favourite among first club-goers and then the wider public, sales rocketed. It replaced 'Boom Boom Pow' at number one and stayed there for eight weeks. This meant that the band had been at the top of the charts with one song or the other for twenty consecutive weeks.

The band was suddenly making chart history. The frenzy around them was becoming ever wilder. When 'Gotta' was featured on the opening episode of *The Oprah Winfrey Show*, it reached an even wider audience. The song was the soundtrack to a spectacular 'flashmob' surprise for the show's host. Some 20,000 people took part in the stunt, on Chicago's Magnificent Mile. Will, a friend of Winfrey, was

Taking the planet by storm on their E.N.D World Tour 2010. [Right] Walking on air in Paris.

A hit in the style stakes as well as the charts: Will.i.am is known for his eclectic fashion sense.

Not afraid to push the boundaries: Will.i.am sports a LEGO hat.

Mentor, co-star and friend: Will.i.am and Cheryl Cole share an unbreakable bond.

The pair perform together at London's O2 Arena in May 2010.

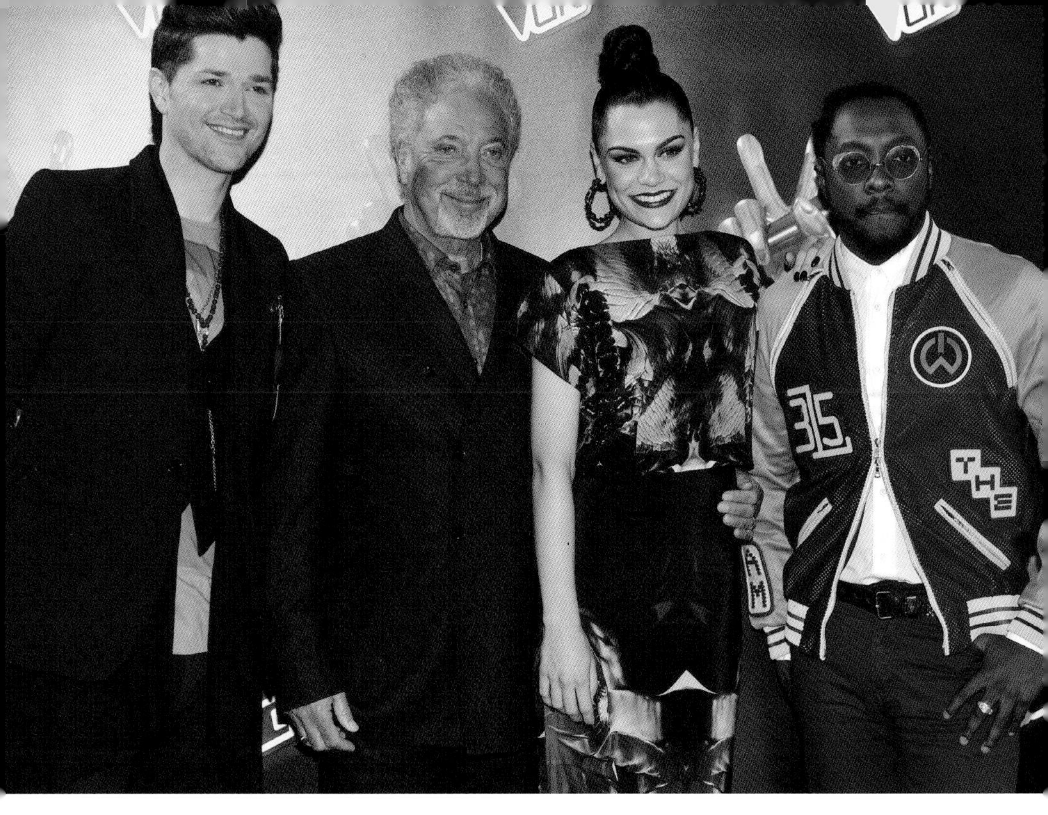

[Above] Will.i.am with his fellow panellists at the launch of *The Voice*.
[Below] The presenters join the line-up.

Will.i.am's involvement in the Diamond Jubilee Concert saw him rubbing shoulders with royalty.

Dazzling the Jubilee crowds with
[right] Jessie J and [below] Stevie Wonder.

Britain's guest of honour: Will.i.am carries the Olympic torch in the run-up to the London 2012 Olympics.

so proud to have been at the centre of such a memorable opening to the television queen's new series. The band's interaction with the audience, spearheaded as ever by Will's charisma, took an already remarkable spectacle to new heights. 'There's something really special when you take an audience and, instead of just being passive and watching, you invite them to participate,' said director Michael Gracey. 'That's why it was so magical for both parties. Two groups of people came together to create something that neither of them could have done alone.'

The band performed the hit song at a number of other prestigious, high-profile events. These included the Super Bowl XLIV in Miami, Florida, and at the Grammys. However, none were as eye-catching as the Oprah flash-mob. Here was a thousands-strong, visual spectacle that defined perfectly the themes of positivity and unity that have been so important to Will throughout his life.

When *The E.N.D.* was released, this magnificent momentum was maintained. It hit the number-one spot in America and was praised by the critics. This time, *Rolling Stone* was admiring of the work, and focused on Will in particular. 'It's easy to make fun of will.i.am, an LA operator who has become a ubiquitous pop-culture presence, turning up on red carpets and appearing on CNN in hologram form,' it wrote. 'On *The E.N.D.*, he does the musical equivalent of the CNN shtick: doing silly, gratuitous, cool things with technology just because, you know, it can be done. As often as not the results are dumb. And that's an awfully good thing.'

Meanwhile, *The Los Angeles Times* focused on 'I Gotta Feeling', and stated: 'It's impossible to begrudge the high. Yes, the song says, this is a sloppy party. But it's one where you're welcome. So come on in.' Only the *Independent* sneered, arguing of the album's songs: 'To call these slim sketches songs is to bestow a dignity they don't deserve'. Will could easily overlook the insult, as once again the wider and truer jury of public opinion was offering an enthusiastic verdict on the album. *The E.N.D.* was proving to be a new beginning.

Will saw the album as a reflection of the post-album era. 'It's a diary ... of music that at any given time, depending on the inspiration, you can add to it,' he said, quoted on the band's official website. 'What is an album when you put twelve songs on iTunes and people can pick at it like scabs? That's not an album. There is no album anymore'.

To which genre did this multigenre 'diary' belong? Will described it as 'a lot of dance stuff, real melodic, electronic, soulful. We call it, like, electric static funk, something like that.' Whichever name one chose to apply to the rich, multiflavoured smorgasbord that the album served up, there was no doubting its commercial viability. While Will's solo career had, thus far, been a more indulgent project, his Black Eyed Peas manifesto was one that had its eye firmly on the market.

And the market had an eye firmly on the band – intensely so in the cases of some of the band's more dedicated fans. While in Japan, Will had an encounter with a fan who had paid close attention to his song 'Boom Boom Pow', which he later recounted to *NME* magazine. 'In Japan this girl comes up and says, "I reckon in 'Boom Boom Pow', you say boom 101 times".' Will assumed she was winding him up. 'I was like, "Yeah, right," but said, "Thank you so much for listening to the song." I got back on the train, counted my booms and she was right,' he said. 'She counted all the booms.'

This is just the sort of obsessive attention to detail that Will admires. He had, albeit momentarily, just encountered a fan very much like himself. However, as he and his band's army of fans swelled ever wider, there would also be trolls attracted to them for the wrong reason. Will's band was about to become the target for one of showbiz's most notorious critics. By the time their clash was over, things would have become very serious.

*

There is nothing quite like a celebrity spat to get the public talking. Feuds of the famous are loved by the media and their readers and viewers alike. Will found himself caught up in one such spat in 2009, when he had a very public falling-out with the flamboyant, opinionated celebrity blogger, Perez Hilton. Hilton, whose real name is Mario Armando Lavandeira, Jr, is no stranger to controversy. He launched a blog, eventually called Perez Hilton, in 2001, the light-hearted wordplay in the title reflecting both his Latino heritage and his friendship with socialite Paris Hilton. However, while Hilton became a firm supporter of several stars – and a personal friend of some, too – he has also become notorious for his feuds with some celebrities. His combination of catty posts about celebrities' appearances and some hard-nosed news revelations have made him a contentious and polarizing figure. Meanwhile, his notoriety has risen.

Therefore, Will was far from the first famous person to become embroiled in an argument with Hilton. His clash with the blogger was, though, a particularly spectacular one. The problem started at an after-show party following a music-award show in Toronto. According to Hilton, Fergie had approached him at the party to ask him why he was being so critical of her on his blog. Hilton had also been dismissive of the band's latest single.

Hilton's literary style rarely pulled any punches, so confrontations such as these are not unheard of. However, many celebrities prefer to make their complaints remotely, or via their representatives. Few are willing to complain directly to their critics. Following this conversation, says Hilton on his website, Will approached him later in the evening and told him: 'I need you to never write about my band on your website again.'

Following an exchange of words, Hilton says he was attacked outside the venue. 'I was in shock,' said the blogger in a video post. 'Nothing like this has ever happened before.' He accused The Black Eyed Peas' manager Liborio Molina of the assault. Hilton also tweeted his side of the story, in a dramatic 4 a.m. posting. 'I was assaulted by will.i.am of the Black Eyed Peas and his security guards. I am bleeding. Please, I need to file a police report. No joke.' On his blog, Hilton claimed that one of Will's managers had hit him 'two or three times'.

Will hit back in a video blog: 'This is very wrong ... that you are tweeting that I did this,' he said. 'Once again, you are disrespecting me [and] all that I stand for.' He claimed that Hilton shouted at him: 'You're not a f**king artist ... you're a f**king f*ggot.'

Hilton confirmed, in an interview with the Associated Press, that he had indeed used these words. Hilton said: 'He was like, "You need to respect me". He was in my face. He was obviously trying to intimidate me and scare me. I was like, "I don't need to respect you". I don't respect you and I did say this, and I knew that it would be the worst thing I could possibly say to him because he was acting the way he was. I said, "You know what, I don't respect you and you're gay and stop being such a faggot.'"

Video footage, obtained by the TMZ website, backed up that these words were used and that they proved the inflammatory moment in the incident. In its frame-by-frame analysis of the footage, TMZ correctly reports that after the 'faggot' word was used to describe Will, 'the scene suddenly turns chaotic – and in the mess someone punches Perez in the face.'

As the war of words continued via the Internet, the media followed the story closely. To clarify the issue at the heart of the dispute, Will stated to Hilton: 'I didn't hit you. I told you that I didn't like the fact that you disrespected us. It's cool to have your opinion.'

Hilton, in turn, denied that, saying: 'I would never make something like this up, or try to use something like this for press, because I don't need it.' This reflected the widespread allegation that, in taking to the Internet to complain rather than contacting law-enforcement authorities, Hilton had been more interested in attention. 'I called the police

BEFORE I Tweeted about it,' Hilton responded. 'They were not showing up. I felt helpless.'

As the media and public became ever more entertained by the controversy, American broadcaster Ryan Seacrest involved himself in the dispute, inviting both parties on to his radio show to give their sides of the story and clear it up. He tweeted: 'I am sorting thru this drama with perez and will.i.am! Have u heard? Perez need u to call radio show to clear this up. Will caall radio show [sic].'

There was plenty of sympathy for Will in the wake of the incident. Hilton's blog had been bitchy about so many celebrities over the years that some people felt he was due a bit of payback. The nature of this genre of blogging – criticism made from the safety of the computer keyboard – had enraged plenty. Kelly Clarkson, the original winner of *American Idol*, for instance, stated on Astral Radio, Toronto that she felt no sympathy for Hilton. 'You're mean to children! No one's going to pity you,' she said. 'I do not think violence is the answer, but what do you expect? I'm surprised it hasn't happened already. I'm thinking how much did will.i.am pay his manager to do that?' The musician John Mayer also attacked Hilton and his handling of the episode. Others made more measured statements. Kate Dailey, writing on the *Daily Beast* website, described Hilton as 'a churlish gadfly', and noted that he had ridiculed people on his blog for years. However, she felt this did not justify violence: 'Did he deserve a beating? No: no one does.'

Hilton eventually filed a lawsuit alleging battery and intentional infliction of emotional distress and sought unspecified damages in excess of $25,000, but the assault charge against Molina was dropped after the manager issued a written apology to the blogger in November. 'I apologize for what I did on June 22 of 2009, even though you engaged in highly offensive comments,' read the statement. 'I acknowledge that these kinds of issues should not be resolved through a physical response.'

As part of the agreement, Molina also agreed not to contact Hilton except through his lawyer, not to carry any weapons for twelve months and not to come within 100 yards of the nightclub where the dispute took place. He was also obliged to donate $500 to a charity. The final word on the saga goes to Molina himself, who said: 'I think everything that needed to be said has pretty much been said. Yes, I do regret the whole night.'

*

If the Hilton episode had shaken Will during the latter months of 2009, he would have further tests ahead of him. None would affect his band, though. Lest we lose sight of this, 2010 was a significant year for The Black Eyed Peas. In terms of record sales they broke further records, the band was nominated for six Grammy awards, of which they won three: Best Pop Vocal Album, Best Performance by a Duo or Group and Best Video. A month after landing those gongs, they performed a surprise concert in Times Square.

Some of the concerts they performed around the world during that year were enormous. For instance, in Canada they performed at the Festival d'été de Québec. Held at the Plains of Abraham, the event attracted a crowd of 120,000 fans. The enormous audience made for a stunning sight for Will and the band. Taboo felt as if the atmosphere of the evening created an 'eighth wonder of the world'. These were heady times for them all.

They released their sixth studio album, *The Beginning*. It was more frivolously themed than *The E.N.D.* had been, and all the better for it as far as many listeners were concerned. It's lead single, 'The Time (Dirty Bit)' was released in November and became the band's ninth Top 10 hit in America. Several critics slammed the album, with *The New York Times* declaring it 'a much lesser record than *The E.N.D.*', the *Chicago Times* declaring its tracks 'dull', and revealing of the band's 'limitations'. The *Guardian*, though, said 'most of the songs hit the mark', and gave it three out of five stars. Will preferred to concentrate on the album's substantial sales, which quickly passed the three million mark. Describing the album's overall style, he told *The New York Times*, it was an electro album, adding: 'Electro is today's disco – making electronic music not for the sake of selling it but for sharing it and touring around the world DJing.' By now, album releases from the band had become major moments in the pop-culture calendar.

Another highlight of the year came in South Africa, where they played at the opening ceremony concert for the football World Cup finals. Over two billion people around the world watched the show on television. 'I Gotta Feeling' had rarely felt more relevant to its surroundings as the multi-racial and multi-national crowd in the stadium jumped and danced to the song, which became an apt soundtrack to the tournament's home: post-apartheid South Africa.

Will continued to campaign for racial equality wherever he travelled. He also encouraged others to take up their own mantles, as when he helped jolly Taboo into speaking out against fresh immigration laws passed in Arizona. With Latinos a prime target of the law's enforcers, Taboo was the right man to take a stand against the laws. It just needed another of those famous Will pep talks to seal the deal. 'Ask yourself this, Tab: look in the mirror and ask yourself, "Do you look illegal?"', was how Will put it. Taboo said he 'had never felt so moved to do something' as he did after that conversation. He would record a song that put into words and music how he felt.

Alongside him as he made the song would be two of Cheryl Cole's backing singers. That was the most tangible impact Cole made on Taboo's career. Her impact on Will's was, and continues to be, far more significant. Thanks to his professional relationship with her, Will had some choppy waters ahead.

6 The Cole Factor

She is one of the most talked about British female celebrities of the last ten years, often described as 'the nation's sweetheart', and yet a woman who has been convicted of assault occasioning actual bodily harm following a scrap in a nightclub toilet. Her combination of glamour and heartache, triumph and disaster makes Cheryl Cole's story irresistible. In recent years, her career and life have become increasingly entwined with those of Will. He was first drawn to work with her not, as some might assume, due to her stunning good looks, but for a rather less discussed aspect of Cole: 'Her personality,' he told *ES* magazine, going on to describe her as, 'Charming, approachable, adorable, sweet, broken, fragile, strong.' As for Cheryl, she was in turn drawn to Will as a manager by his mind. 'He's a genius,' she says. 'He has a genius mind.'

Some commentators have attempted to conjure a

romantic dimension to Will's relationship with Cole. However, the truth is far more fascinating than that. Indeed, his management of and relationship with Cheryl Cole makes for one of the most controversial chapters of his career to date. Apart from rumours of romance, he has both been lauded as the mastermind behind Cole's every success and blamed as the cause of her every failure. It is in his involvement with her that we see the substantial powers that are ascribed to Will by both his fans and critics: few people, it seems, think that Will is a moderate or mediocre force. Rather, he is always cast as a force of nature, causing either triumph or disaster. The truth of the matter is rather more complicated and ambiguous than that.

We start the story with just such an effusive statement, made by Cole herself. The former Girls Aloud star credits Will with the very fact that she has a solo career at all. As ever, Will's positive, encouraging nature rings true. 'It was actually him that convinced me to do a solo record,' she told the Popjustice website. 'I never would have done a solo record without him. At the time, I would have had a family. At the time, I was still married! But it was actually Will saying to us, "You know you're going to do a solo record, right?", and I was saying, "I don't want to, not yet".'

However, Will won the day and encouraged her to do it. He then went a step further, asking if he could work with her on it. 'I think you should – you need to,' he told Cole. 'I'm excited. I want to be involved with it.'

Cole was first drawn to the idea of working with Will when she saw him interviewed on television. He was asked which UK artists he would most like to work with and replied: 'Cheryl Cole and U2'. Cole was touched, but also amused by his interest. 'I did have a little chuckle to me'self,' she recalled later.

So Cole took little convincing to get Will on board for her solo material. He took part in her debut album, *3 Words*, which was released in October 2009. Will was the executive producer and also contributed backing vocals to four songs. These included the album's titular opener, the writing of which he had also been involved in. The album was recorded in California, New York and London.

Will found that working with Cole was 'like working with somebody who I've known for a long time'. Asked to sum up what she was like in the studio, he said: 'She's not just a great singer and a beautiful woman, but a very talented writer – a great lyricist'. For Cole, all too often dismissed as merely a glamorous woman whose looks are almost solely responsible for her success, these words were most encouraging. This was what she had waited so long to hear.

An insight was offered into their working relationship

when they were interviewed together on a one-off UK chat show devoted to her in the winter of 2009. Cole recalled how she was 'Flattered, extremely flattered, that he even knew who I was,' when they decided to work together. She said that 'Will's gentle persuasion' had 'pushed me over the edge' in her decision to go solo. However, when she first entered the studio to work with Will, she was, she admitted, 'terrified'.

Will's first task for Cole was a lyrical one. He played her the music to the tune 'Heaven', and told her to go home and write some lyrics for it. Cole found the experience extremely nerve-wracking, but suspected Will was not aware of that. He corrected her, telling her he was aware of her anxiety. Indeed, back in the studio, when he noted her frame of mind he began to prepare himself for the lyrics to be poor. So, when she began to sing them, he said: 'Wow! There's no reason to be shy – that's the bomb!' One can almost sense the positive, encouraging energy that Will must have created in the studio.

It was positive energy that was reflected in the album's reception and chart progress. Many critics lavished the album with praise, and it debuted at number one in the UK album charts. *Attitude* magazine concluded that Will had hit the nail on the head with his work with Cole's solo debut, calling it: 'Very hip, very now and ultimately very Cheryl'.

Will's professional relationship with Cole deepened the following year, when he invited her to join The Black Eyed Peas tour. She impressed the band members, who were taken aback by her beauty and her down-to-earth, Geordie attitude to her celebrity. It is hard, after all, to imagine a woman of such glamour managing to maintain such an everyday approach to life were she, say, Californian.

At the end of her warm-up set on the first date in Dublin, Will rapped: 'Cheryl Cole's so sexy'. He and Cole were becoming increasingly inseparable, prompting his Black Eyed Peas bandmates to tease him onstage about their relationship, singing: 'Will and Cheryl sitting in a tree, k-i-s-s-i-n-g'. In truth, this was just a bit of banter. The fans mostly realized this, but the rumourmongers of the World Wide Web, not to mention the ladies and gentlemen of the mainstream media, were less in on the joke. They therefore read more into it than was intended, all of which made for more fascination.

*

The next chapter of Will's professional relationship with Cole followed the conclusion of her time on The Black Eyed Peas tour. Cole invited Will to appear alongside her in the judges' houses phase of the 2010 UK *X Factor* series. He did not take long to decide he would accept the invitation. However, initially, his management team was less than thrilled, complaining that it would be impossible to fit such a commitment into Will's schedule.

'What you talking about my schedule for?' Will asked them. 'Just put it in the schedule!' This would give Will a foot in the door of reality-television contests – a genre responsible for a significant slice of the pop world's turnover – as well as bringing his personal fame to a whole new audience.

For the show, he was a welcome addition. Past judges' houses assistants included 1980s pop star Sinitta, Westlife's least popular member Kian Egan, and other, even less famous 'stars'. Will would, at this stage, constitute one of the series' biggest 'assistant' names to date, paving the way for the likes of Kylie Minogue and Robbie Williams to follow in his footsteps.

As Will prepared for *The X Factor* experience he had mixed feelings. He was looking forward immensely to working with Cole and to witnessing the performance of the remaining contestants in her girls category. He did not fear that they would disagree much, as he believed that Cole, 'unlike a lot of artists has an ear ... and a nose'. So there was plenty of positivity to anticipate.

At the same time, though, Will felt troubled to be stepping inside the circus. As one who had based his career on a principle of encouragement, positive energy and kindness, he felt uncomfortable with some of the rougher edges of *The X Factor*. Clearly, the catty remarks of Simon Cowell were not ones that Will would feel well disposed towards. However, his misgivings went both wider and deeper than that. He felt ill at ease with the very nature of a process that played with the emotions of aspiring artists purely to make breathtaking television. As he stepped into Simon Cowell's world, Will vowed to himself that he would be as true to his beliefs as he could be.

In the past, the judges' houses phase of the contest had been held at locations as glamorous as Australia, California and Barcelona. Cole had chosen somewhere closer to home: Coworth Park in Ascot, Berkshire. After Cole had been unveiled as their mentor, the girls were excited to discover who would be her famous assistant. After the customary dramatic pause, Cole said: 'It's Mr will.i.am'. As the contestants jumped, applauded and screamed, Will sauntered down the stairs in his usual cool style and said: 'What's up, girls?'

Once the performances began, Will noticed that there were, in fact, two performances going on at any given time. One was the singing of the song itself, the second was the performance of, 'Oh, look at me! I'm going to be on TV'. This aspect of the show fascinated him but did not make him any the more enamoured by the genre.

No contestant epitomized this dichotomy more than Katie Waissel. The polarizing drama queen of the entire series, Waissel broke down during her rendition of 'Smile', and generally milked the entire audition for as much attention and theatre as she could get. Will, though, defended her to Cole. 'She seems good', he said. Of Gamu Nhengu, another controversial contestant, he said 'nice tone'. Cher Lloyd, like Waissel, had to interrupt her performance with a tearful breakdown. Will sat uncomfortably as Cole comforted Lloyd. Little could he have known, at this stage, that Lloyd, who also messed-up her second crack at the song, would make it through to the final, where she would duet with him. 'Wow', he said after Lloyd's tearful, despairing exit. He tried to remind himself that the girl he had just seen in such torment was 'sixteen years old'. His serious and deflated air was palpable. Had his fears about the format been realized?

After the auditions had taken place, Will looked back over the experience. 'It was cool, you know, it was harder than it looked,' he told *The X Factor* website. 'Cos every single one of the girls were great singers.' This created a difficult situation for Will as he advised Cole which of the acts to put through to the live shows, and which to send home. He felt that – whatever the choices Cole and he had made – they would be criticized by those watching at home. 'It's hard, you know – being judged for judging.' He added, though, that the decision was eased because 'you just can't ignore magic dust'. Cole added that Will's advice had been 'vital'. She said that she 'trusted his instinct ... above my own'.

However, for seasoned observers of Will it seemed that all was not quite well. The normally talkative and energetic man was replaced by one lacking 'fizz', a man who seemed almost perplexed and deflated by the experience. It was hard to imagine at this stage that Will would soon be representing Cole as she herself was sucked further into the *X Factor* universe, only to be embarrassingly spat out.

That episode took place over the Atlantic, where Simon Cowell was fulfilling a longstanding dream by leaving his place as a judge on Simon Fuller's *American Idol*, in order to launch his own *X Factor* franchise in the States. For Cowell, this was the biggest risk of his television career to date. His already notoriously obsessive attention to detail would be tightened all the more. For him, getting the judging panel right for the show was absolutely vital.

It is Simon Cowell's belief that *The X Factor* is more about the drama of the judges than it is about the contestants. So he wanted the perfect chemistry on the panel. Which is how Will became embroiled in the hullabaloo, over Cowell's invitation to Cole to be one of his fellow judges in America.

Having accepted the role, as Cole prepared to move to the States, Will joined her new management team. Cole arrived in America in May 2011. She was welcomed by Will and he reportedly threw a party to introduce her to some of his key contacts. By August, having tired of life in hotels, Cole was reported to have moved into Will's home in Hollywood. By this time it was already clear that she was not entirely comfortable in the US.

Fate was already pointing towards a showdown between Will and Cowell over the former's client. However, Will spoke in encouraging terms about both Cole and Cowell. He predicted that the UK *X Factor* show, which Cole and Cowell had left behind for the American launch, would struggle to replace either judge. 'I don't think there is much doubt that Simon and Cheryl are the main two guys,' he told the *Sun*. 'Simon is the glue that holds everything together and people love to watch him, and Cheryl is like a queen in the UK. They are both irreplaceable.'

He continued to be positive – glowingly so – about *The X Factor*, as the series he had made a cameo appearance in rolled on. 'I love *X Factor*,' he said. The two acts he selected for praise were both in Cole's category. For him, Cher Lloyd was the queen of the series, and he backed her to win. However, the pint-sized pop princess could only manage fourth place. The highest finisher of Cole's category was

Rebecca Ferguson, another act that Will had plenty of time for. 'You'd think Rebecca was hanging out with Marvin Gaye every day, she has so much soul,' he said. 'I would love to work with [Ferguson and Lloyd]. If I was starting off and went on that show, I'd never make it through as the talent is of such a high standard.'

However, positive words about the franchise were about to leave Will's vocabulary. Everything was about to go terribly wrong for Cole, and Will was about to be handed a crash course in both the politics of the entertainment industry and the scale of that challenges that artists' representatives can face. His client's dream of cracking America as a judge on *The X Factor* fell at the first hurdle.

During her first day as a judge, in the auditions in Los Angeles, Cole appeared lost. Her outfit and hairstyle was also criticized – with one wag comparing her look to that of *Star Wars* creature Chewbacca. Over the next three days of auditions, Cole did not improve her form enough to deflect Cowell's growing sense of unease. Cole seemed, said Cowell, later, explaining her departure, 'bewildered'. She was booed by the audience at one point, had minimal rapport with her fellow judges, and became tearful when she was asked to repeat herself. It was all a world away from her reign on the UK show, on which she had appeared almost majestic.

As the decision was reached to replace Cole, Will was

thrust into the complex, tense and financially significant negotiations surrounding her removal from the series. Cole had signed a £1.2 million contract to judge on the show, so the stakes were high as negotiations began.

Initially, according to Tom Bower's biography of Simon Cowell, an offer was made to Cole – not through Will but another of her agents, Seth Friedman – of $2m to pay up her US contract, and a further £2m to return to the UK *X Factor*. Cowell's camp indicated they wanted a swift resolution. Friedman was then joined in the negotiations by Will. First, he requested equity in the *X Factor* franchise for Cole, in addition to any other deal. Cowell responded that the equity was not his to offer, but instead offered to up her fee for the UK series, include the potential for bonuses for ratings, and agreed to award her a credit as an executive producer of the series. As he put it, he was making a generous offer in order to resolve the negotiation 'cleanly and quickly'.

Will replied that he would go away for a while, 'and consider other options'. According to Bower's much-discussed biography of Simon Cowell, Will accused Cowell of undermining Cole by reducing the volume of her microphone. According to Bower, Cowell felt that Will was 'riding his own ego', rather than working in the best interests of Cole. In turn, Will insisted that the opposite was true.

When details of the episode were leaked to the TMZ website, Cowell complained: 'Will doesn't understand the pressures we're under.' While Cowell's aides complained that Will did not realize that they were trying to help him and Cole, Cowell said that he thought he and Will 'had a good relationship'.

Cowell's frustration with Will at this stage is understandable. Will's client was being offered a lavish package. However, Will's perspective should also be considered fairly. His client had been enormously upset by her departure from the show. Having moved to America months ahead of the series, uprooting her life and replacing members of her team, she had been axed after just four days in the new job. Furthermore, Will was aware that Cowell's empire and the Fox television network were, between them, sitting on billions of dollars. Thus, it could be that the opening offers made to Cole were not as generous as they might appear to the outside observer.

Will was determined to fight hard for his client and not to be cowed by the combined power of Cowell and Fox TV. His steadfast approach almost reaped a complete turnaround as, behind the scenes, members of the Fox network and the Freemantle Media production company were actively lobbying for Cole to return to the US show as soon as possible. Freemantle's Cecile Frot-Coutaz prepared to contact Cole to invite her back, and Will to instruct him to take Cole to the American embassy in London to obtain a new work permit.

However, Will was not about to fall at their feet. He asked whether the offer for Cole to return was, in fact, a trick. He wondered whether he and Cole were being led into a situation whereby, if she refused the offer, Team Cowell could refuse to pay her. Cowell was frustrated and asked Will whether Cole wanted to return or not. Will replied with an ambiguous: 'That isn't your concern.' In the end the negotiations were concluded successfully, but with an agreement that did not include Cole's return to either the American or UK *X Factor* show. For now, at least, her professional relationship with Cowell was over, and she needed Will's support more than ever.

Throughout the drama, Cole, usually comfortable with publicity, had remained publicly silent. Aside from some newspaper stories quoting 'sources close to' her – the authenticity of which were open to debate – she had not said a word. Instead, it was Will who began the public 'rehabilitation' of his client. It was no surprise that, despite the huge disappointment and ignominy Cole had suffered, Will spoke in optimistic terms. 'She always comes back stronger, and she always comes back bigger,' he told *Heat* magazine. 'Cheryl has been through rougher things than this, so this is going to be no problem for her. *The X Factor* is not the only way for Cheryl to break the US, it's not like it's the only show on television.'

At this stage, relations between Will and Cowell were, certainly in public, still essentially warm. Asked if Cowell was to blame for Cole's humiliating departure, Will resisted the temptation to blame *The X Factor* boss alone. 'It's easy to imagine Simon as this one-man empire, but that's not the case. He has people he needs to answer to and sometimes his hands are going to be tied,' said Will. It was a sentence that at once absolved and belittled Cowell. Given Will's intelligence, one suspects this was not accidental. However, he continued in more friendly terms, saying, 'I can only tell you what I have seen first-hand: that's a guy who deeply cares for her.'

Meanwhile, Will preferred to look to Cole's future, predicting that in the months ahead she would be working with some top musical artists, including Rihanna, Katy Perry, Usher, 'and of course the Peas'.

His positivity over Cole's future is classic Will, of course. Few celebrities are as powered by positivity as he is. From his childhood games in the playground at school, to his car-park pep talk with Taboo, and onwards, Will has always radiated upbeat energy, and has also developed an almost Olympian skill at looking on the bright side of any situation. If you ever find yourself in a troubled or despairing situation, you could do a lot worse than to run it past Will, whose mind seems to be a factory of bright-side perspectives.

These powers are mostly to be applauded, of course. However, in the case of Cole's *X Factor* failure, his 'silver lining' of that particular cloud stretches credibility. For Cole, this had been a devastating blow. She had staked so much on making it on the American *X Factor* – leaving her country, much of her original management and her solo career all behind – placing all her eggs in one basket. To have those eggs hurled out of the basket almost immediately was embarrassing for Cole as a person and, potentially, devastating to her professionally.

When he joined her US management team, Will had been full of bombast: 'She's got a bright future ahead – no question,' he said. Therefore, the hit that Cole took in being ejected from *The X Factor* not only struck her, but also Will, who had told friends that he was so confident he would stake his reputation on making her American dream come true.

As well as talking *up* Cole, Will attempted to raise her stature by talking down the circus from which she had been ejected. He began to argue that she had wasted her time on *The X Factor*. 'Cheryl is a great artist and performer and to see that go away just for TV – it wasn't cool. It was a waste of talent,' he told the *Daily Star Sunday*. He added that by concentrating on television rather than music, she had 'abandoned her basics'.

He also slammed the team behind the UK show for what he saw as the failure of 2010 *X Factor* graduate Cher Lloyd's career. 'She should have been huge,' he said of Lloyd, who had been Cole's act during that series. Of course, part of his dismissal of *The X Factor* was due to his forthcoming starring role on what would be its UK primetime Saturday-night rival. *The Voice*, he argued, was quite a contrast to *The X Factor*. The show on which he would appear would, he said, 'honour what music was originally about and take it back full circle to what it was always meant to be, The Voice.' What better way to gain the last laugh in this sorry saga than to make the show that Cowell dreaded a big success?

Meanwhile, Will took stock. He admitted that 'it was hard' to deal with the Cole fall-out. He had not been prepared for the issue to arise as it had, and he had to learn fast the best way to respond to such episodes. Looking back later, he felt he had learned well. 'Since the American *X Factor* stuff I've learned a lot – about myself and the music industry,' he said.

While Will and his client were individually shaken, their relationship seemed not to be. One of the first times that Cole was seen in public following the saga, was alongside

Will in Cannes, France. Cole was even said to have cooked meals for Will during his stint on *The Voice*. The Geordie also taught him British slang terms, to help settle him into the country better. They found that, emotionally, they were each other's greatest source of solace. 'At first it would bring my emotions down,' said Will, 'but now when things come up we giggle and laugh about them together'.

If Will continues to mentor and manage Cole and other artists there will be more tough times in the future as they navigate the rollercoaster path of show business. Being able to laugh, or at least smile, through the downturns will make the upturns all the sweeter.

More recently, Will has been less charitable and philosophical in discussing Simon Cowell's role, taking a very thinly veiled swipe at him during an interview with the *Sun* newspaper. 'There are English guys that go to America and it's hard for them. Let's take Cheryl Cole, for example. She went and did a TV show and it was hard for her. And it wasn't hard for her because of an American. It was hard for her because of a Brit. Now that's kind of weird, isn't it?'

In an interview with the *Sunday Mirror*, he was even more mischievous towards Cowell, saying he hoped that Cole would join him on *The Voice* one day. 'I mean, why not? That would really p*ss the big man off, wouldn't it?' Earlier, in response to Cowell's statement that Cole 'missed' being on *The X Factor*, and would '100 per cent' be welcomed back to the fold, Will was once again rather dismissive of the music mogul and his empire. 'Cheryl won't do *X Factor*,' he told the *Mirror*. 'Why does she need it? Why are you going to make someone else rich? Cheryl needs her own show.'

Significantly, during his defence of Cole's *Voice* appearance, Will seemed to be managing the public's expectations of his client's ability to crack the American market. His previously bold assertion that she would make it big in America, despite the *X Factor* setback, seemed to have been knocked. 'America's a weird place right now, in terms of breaking,' he said. 'I don't know who is breaking America right now.'

Will could not resist a cheeky dig at Cowell when he spoke with the *Evening Standard*'s Craig McLean. The journalist persistently pressed Will to make an outrageous statement about Cowell, to no avail. He suggested to Will that Cowell had been less than honest in his handling of Cole's *X Factor* fall. Will stared into McLean's eyes, clenched his fist and moved it up and down, in a fairly clear simulation of masturbation. 'Wish you could print hand gestures,' Will said, as his fist moved up and down. When McLean told Will how he was interpreting his hand gesture, Will remained teasing. 'Nah, like, whatever dude,' he said.

Pressed one more time to reveal what really happened between him, Cowell and Cole, Will said: 'I wish I could show you. But I'm not that kind of guy.'

Some of the above anti-Cowell bravado had as much to do with promoting a rivalry between his new home, *The Voice*, and Cowell's empire, as it did any genuine remaining bitterness. Will has, more recently, seemed keen to put the entire US *X Factor* saga in the past. He did his best to consign it to the history books by speaking about his client's future. 'The Cheryl that we know now is different from the one we're going to know ten years from now,' he said. 'It was ten years ago that me and the Black Eyed Peas wrote "Where is the Love?"' he continued, in a clear reference to how far the band had come since then. 'I'm planning a future for Cheryl in that way. Madonna is Madonna. You don't want Cheryl to be Madonna, you want Cheryl to be Cheryl.'

Final word on the *X Factor* saga goes to Cheryl, who showed there were no hard feelings between her and her manager when she described Will as a 'genius', and promised to take him for a special night out in the North East of England. 'No matter where I am in the world, someone always comes up and says Newcastle is one of the best nights out,' she said. 'I'm taking Will to Bigg Market for a kebab. I'm planning to take him out up there. He took me to downtown LA. That's where he's from, Boyle Heights. I'll have to show him what the North East has to offer.'

It would be fascinating to know what he made of the 'Toon' experience. She also took him for good old-fashioned fish and chips in London. She has, more recently, described him as 'an honorary Brit'. Across the Atlantic, when Cole celebrated her twenty-ninth birthday in Las Vegas, Will played a DJ set during the knees-up at the XS nightclub.

Naturally, their intense relationship has prompted continued speculation that they are a romantic item. As we have seen, Will's bandmates have even humorously encouraged this theory. With a wider fascination over Will's private life, there has been much interest in just how close he and his client are.

As for Cole, she speaks fondly of Will. When asked by an interviewer for the *Guardian* newspaper what quality she most admires in a person, her instantaneous reply was: 'Loyalty. Someone who is always there, not judging you, regardless of what situation you're in.' She volunteered Will as an example of such a person. 'We call each other family,' she says. It is that, familial, description that comes closest to summing up the bond. They are more like brother and sister than anything else. Will was asked by *Q* magazine if he was, in fact, Cole's fella. 'Fella? Fella? I like that,' he said, 'that's a good word for a new squeeze.' However, he quickly scotched the perception. Saying that while 'on the Internet we are married with children', in reality 'people know we are occasional work colleagues'.

In denying the rumours of romance, he was careful not to downplay his admiration for Cole. 'Cheryl's awesome', he said, adding: 'That accent I would die for'. He recounted how he sometimes shows her something unpleasant on the Internet, merely to get the chance to hear her say, in her Geordie accent, 'That's disgusting!'.

Elsewhere, during an interview with the Sun, he was more direct in his denial. 'Yes, Cheryl and I are both in love – with music', he said. 'That's why we get on so well. Those rumours were hilarious. I've been lucky to work with her. I think I've helped to bring out the best in her.'

Cole, too, denies the suggestion. In her case, the denials are more annoyed than witty. 'Of course that's the natural thing people go to,' she told *ES* magazine. 'Heaven forbid you should have any other kind of relationship with someone from the opposite sex.'

Meanwhile, he found himself having to jump to his client's defence once again when she appeared on *The Voice*. In May 2012, Cheryl sang her new single, 'Call My Name', on the show's semi-final. She had promised that, in keeping with the overall ethos of the show, she would not mime her vocals during her performance. Onlookers said that Cole had looked to Will for 'reassurance' at several points in the song.

For the appearance she wore a colourful outfit and her dance moves were dramatic, including a 'swan dive'. Many viewers complained on Twitter that Cole appeared to be miming. However, her publicist insisted otherwise. 'She sang live with a backing track', said the spokesperson. A 'source' quoted in the *Sun* said: 'It would have been hard for Cheryl to have sung through the whole performance – it was such an energetic dance routine'.

Will, though, was having none of it. He said: 'I was there. She wasn't miming. People say a lot of things.' Elsewhere, he had berated the media for giving Cole 'shit'. He said that they should recognize her true worth: 'She's your royalty, man'. He has even gone as far as comparing her to his all-time inspiration, Michael Jackson. 'Like Michael Jackson, she is a complete perfectionist', he said, in an eyebrow-raising comparison. 'Unless she is 100 per cent happy with something she just won't put it out there.'

As for Cole, she remains enamoured by Will's magical talent. 'I would work with Will for the rest of my career if I could,' she said. 'He is absolutely inspiring, futuristic, creative.'

Perhaps the truth of their bond is that, despite their fame and success, both stars feel emotionally lonely and unsatisfied in some sense. Their professional success has come at the expense of personal happiness. The comfort that their professional journeys and personal bonding has brought to each of them has been significant.

Will had been delighted to see his client on *The Voice*. The way their paths crossed on the show provided a sense of closure after a tough year for both of them due to the *X Factor* USA saga. *The Voice* is an important chapter in Will's life, so let us turn to his successful involvement on the BBC show, how it all started and how it led to Will becoming a much-admired part of the British mainstream, so much so that he got to rub shoulders with the nation's real royalty – and secure a place in the hearts of the public. The Anglophile's love was about to become more requited than ever.

7 *The Voice* and Beyond

Initially, Will was just a viewer of *The Voice* like everyone else. In the Spring of 2011, he had watched the debut American series of the franchise on NBC and absolutely 'loved it'. So he was thrilled when the approach first came for him to appear as a star on the British series, to run in the Spring of 2012. Setting aside any suspicions that he was going to be a harsh, tough-talking judge in the mould of Simon Cowell, in keeping with the producers of the show's wishes, he preferred to refer to himself as 'a coach'.

'Throughout my career when I have coached people, it has always been all about being someone's friend,' he said on the Unreality TV website. 'I want to go about *The Voice* with the same perspective in the sense that a friend is better than being a mentor or coach. I really want to be able to give my team my perspective on the music business.'

From the start, Will wanted to separate himself from

the stereotypical judges of talent shows of recent times. So, in a thinly veiled critique of *The X Factor*, he explained on Digital Spy why he saw *The Voice* as different. 'When singers go on the other shows, you're probably never going to hear from those people again,' he said. 'Why? Because their souls and their whole world has been crushed and they've been embarrassed in front of everybody. This one's different. I want to see every single person that walked off that stage proud and not battered and bruised, because this is their passion.'

Why, in reality, was Will at such great pains to differentiate *The Voice* from its rivals? It was not so much the public he wanted to convince that his show would be better than anything before: he seemed to also want to convince himself of it. Perhaps the only way he could truly relax into his role was to believe that the show he was joining was more sincere than its rivals. So keen was he to make this case that he was even willing to talk down its broadcasting appeal in order to talk up its musical credibility. 'Maybe it doesn't make great TV, but it's gonna make great artists,' he said, in a statement that might have made the production team shuffle uncomfortably when they heard it. 'Do you want TV or do you want artists that are gonna go and perform for people and make people forget about their problems for five minutes in a song? TV's great, but there's lots of it.'

He went even further, with a surprisingly comprehensive swipe at all the judges on the *X Factor* and *Idol* shows. '*The Voice* is different,' he said. 'On one, you have people in the music industry, current and legends, coaching the next generation. The other format you have judges critiquing, giving their opinions on things when they don't really know, other than Randy Jackson on *Idol*. But on *The Voice*, we've all got experience.'

Given that past and present judges on reality talent shows included artists of the not inconsiderable calibre of Paula Abdul, Steven Tyler, Dannii Minogue and Cheryl Cole, Will's statement was quite a blow. Perhaps he had excluded Cole in his mind, given that she had, at this stage, left the reality-television sphere, for the time being at least. Indeed, he admitted that he had sought her counsel for his new job.

Even in explaining this, he could not resist yet another attack on *The Voice*'s rivals. 'I reached out to Cheryl for advice on keeping your cool, having a poker face, the importance of sticking with the singers – it's their dream,' he told Capital FM radio. 'A lot of the times when you have other performers as part of the show, celebrities tend to want the shine so they hog up time. So my whole thing was that I want to do *The Voice*, but I don't want to hog up time to where the singers up there are looking like, "Is this about you guys?"'

Her advice, he felt, had been more than useful, 'Her

information that she gave me was inspirational. Her perspective and experience inspired me.' However, although he sought advice, for Will, the talent search was not to be a new experience – just one transferred into a new context. 'No, this is what I've always done when I'm not performing,' he told the *Radio Times*. 'I'm looking for new acts, I'm mentoring people signed to my label, wherever I am, after a show, when I go to a club. It's just now I'm doing it on a different platform.'

The gimmick for *The Voice* is that the opening auditions are 'blind'. That is to say the coaches sit with their backs to the singer and, if they like what they hear, they can press a button on their chair, which then spins them around so they can see the singer for the first time. The idea being that it is all about the voice of the person, not their look or stage persona. At the end of the song, all the coaches face the singer, but only those who spun round during the performance are allowed to bid to mentor the singer in the next round. As we shall see, the sincerity of this dimension of the show was to be questioned by many viewers and several critics.

Nonetheless, as the countdown to the broadcast of the first episode continued, Will prepared to acquire a new wave of recognition in Britain. While The Black Eyed Peas had for some time been a very popular act here, theirs is the sort of mainstream success that means that far from all of those who can hum along to their biggest hits would be able to tell you the names of any of the band's members, let alone recognize them. *The Voice* would jettison Will directly into the living rooms of a primetime BBC One audience week after week – recognition did not get much more mainstream than that. Will, for all his disdain of Simon Cowell and his shows, was more than aware of how *Pop Idol* and then *The X Factor* had taken Cowell from anonymity to huge fame at record speed. Meanwhile, there was always the risk that the entire project could be a failure, so the stakes were high.

Alongside Will on the show would be three other celebrity coaches: Welsh legend Sir Tom Jones, pop princess Jessie J, and The Script's Danny O'Donoghue. The inclusion of O'Donoghue had proved controversial after he pipped Will Young to the post for the role. Young was furious and Twitter users were aghast, somewhat unkindly renaming him Danny O'Donog-Who? Will suffered no such issues with recognition, though he was new to some viewers. Still, the panel was described as a 'blockbuster line-up' by Will Payne of the *Daily Mirror*.

Will's opening words on the opening episode were familiar: announcing that this was 'not like the traditional, karaoke talent show'. Will was introduced to viewers as the 'founding member of global supergroup The Black Eyed

Peas, seven-time Grammy winner, and established producer, who has collaborated with music's biggest names.' It was a curriculum vitae that, arguably, cast him as the most widely qualified of the coaches. The coaches started the series opener by performing together one of Will's biggest hits: 'I Gotta Feeling'. In a grey-and-white baseball jacket, Will looked pumped-up and slightly nervous. There was much at stake for him.

In the opening audition of the series, Will was the first to press his button and face the contestant. It took him little time to be won over by the sound of Jessica Hammond covering Jessie J's 'Price Tag'. By the end of the song, all four coaches had followed suit, leading each time to much mock-indignant body language from Will.

It was then time for each coach to make their pitch to mentor the contestant. 'So, I would like to work with you,' Will said to Jessica Hammond. 'The way I've worked with Macy, and Michael Jackson ...' O'Donoghue then made a joke about Will name-dropping. This would be just the first of many such quips between the coaches on that topic. 'I would like to have you on my team, we need to make an album, we need to put it out to where it's big, in the UK, America, Brazil, Philippines, Australia, New Zealand, Mexico, Argentina, Russia, Czech Republic, Kazakhstan, Slovakia, Turkey, Poland...' After being – blissfully – interrupted by O'Donoghue, Will concluded by telling Hammond: 'You need to come here, babers'. He then offered to hold her guitar for her: 'I'll be your roadie. I'll be your producer and your roadie.'

As the coaches vied for Hammond to join their team, there was much banter between them. O'Donghue accused Will of being 'like a lobster' (meaning in this context 'loquacious'), while Jessie J implied that Will 'surrounds himself with "yes men"'.

Already it was clear that Will intended to be an electric presence on the show. To some, the chatter between the judges made for slightly awkward viewing. There was a sense that the judges felt less than comfortable performing such contrived roles. To others, the show made for a breath of fresh air in a format that had become bloated and tired due to the excesses of *The X Factor*.

As for Will, despite being the first to back her, he received his first knockback of the series when Hammond, while deliberating on which coach to choose, told him: 'While I appreciate everything you said, I'm a songwriter. I'm only seventeen and from Belfast. Number one hits don't matter to me. Making music and sharing my message is what matters to me.' Wisely, Will did not respond to her meek slap down of his highly commercialized pitch. He had misjudged her core motivation, but not unreasonably so. Perhaps unsurprisingly, given the fact she had auditioned with one of Jessie J's songs, it was she that Hammond chose as her coach. Will would, though, win favour with a number of the contestants in the opening blind auditions round.

Meanwhile, backstage he was reported to have offended BBC executives. According to the *Sun*, Will turned his dressing room at the White City studios into a makeshift music studio, so he could satisfy his creative, workaholic tendencies. Initially, this was welcomed – everyone wanted their star turn to be happy. However, once he had set up his equipment and begun to make music, the sheer volume of his 'mega bass bins' shook up the building, literally and metaphorically. A 'show source' was quoted as saying Will's music had caused serious offence among the suits upstairs. 'Will has some serious bass in there and it was vibrating the walls – you could almost see the dandruff being shaken off their heads,' said the source, providing a memorable image.

A more serious reported bust-up occurred when Will and Jessie J competed to take a singer called Joelle Moses under their wing. Joelle's soulful, slowed-down rendition of Adele's 'Rolling in the Deep' was one of the highlights of the opening auditions. Once again, Will was the first to press his button, followed closely by O'Donoghue. By the end of the audition all four coaches had turned themselves around, with Jessie J the final one to do so. However, when she did turn around, Jessie J broke with etiquette to run onto the stage and embrace the singer. Will pitched himself against Jessie J, saying sardonically: 'I know how to work with good singers, produce them, and stuff like that'. He won the pitch, when Joelle said her 'gut instinct' led her to choose him.

However, Will and Jessie J reportedly also exchanged some unkind words, which were not broadcast. After Jessie J mocked Will's name as containing 'two dashes', he snapped that she was 'Little Miss Jessie'. Will told the press: 'There was one point where my team came in and expressed concerns on the banter between the coaches. I am the most unconfrontational man in the world – it is not my style – but that was the first time they have ever seen that side of me and they were like, "Will, what are you doing?" They pulled me back in the dressing room and told me that I should not be doing that. They said it certainly didn't look like banter.' Furthermore, Will insisted the row was genuine, describing Jessie J and himself as 'hungry people fighting over a steak'.

Such stories frequently appear in the tabloids during reality-television series, some readers take them with a pinch of salt. A more significant claim surfaced in the *Guardian*, which said that Will was comfortably the highest paid of the show's four coaches. The newspaper, a favoured read among many British media figures, claimed that there was a £1 million fund available for the coaches' salaries. It reported that Will had received half of the money – £500,000. The other half was said to be divided between the other three coaches, with Sir Tom Jones taking £250,000. Undisclosed figures put Jessie J as the third-highest paid judge, with O'Donoghue in fourth place, but 'still pulling in six figures'. These figures, though unconfirmed, seem to hold weight. Will was considered the biggest 'catch' by the producers, while O'Donoghue was only a late selection. Four weeks into the series, Will topped the figures for the coach most searched for online. All in all, things were going well for him.

He needed to find a special act to coach. Jaz Ellington was, for many viewers, the most stand-out of Will's acts from the opening auditions. He sang 'The A Team', prompting Will to lead the charge of coaches spinning around. With the other judges having filled their teams already, this astonishing talent was Will's by default. He laughed flamboyantly as he faced Ellington, signalling his soaring confidence that he had discovered a star. He told Ellington it was 'like you just fell out of the sky'. With a very positive atmosphere permeating the studio, Ellington was invited to sing another song. He chose Will's own song, 'Ordinary People'. It was such a powerful performance that it reduced both Will and Jessie J to tears. 'Here comes a little angel with wings', said

Will, summing up the moment. He compared his new act to 'an owl' who can see in the night.

By the end of the first round of auditions, Will believed he had assembled 'the perfect ten' contestants for his team. Among them were Heshima Thompson, barmaid Jenny Jones, Sophie Griffin, J. Marie Cooper, Scouser Jay Norton, Wakefield teenager Frances Wood and Londoner Tyler James. At this stage, for most observers, Ellington and James seemed the cream of Will's crop.

Next up, came the 'Battle Rounds', in which the final forty acts would be reduced to a top twenty. The acts went head-to-head in a 'sing-off', held on a 'boxing ring'-style stage. This made for an intense experience for Will, as he was forced to reduce his top ten to a top five. Among those he took through were Joelle Moses, who edged out Jenny Jones, despite Will feeling Jones was 'smashing it', and Tyler James, who Will said had 'knocked me out with your performance'.

The most intense sing-off by Will's acts came between Jay Norton and Jaz Ellington, who performed 'I Heard it Through the Grapevine'. Between them, they produced a duet of enormous quality. Will told Norton that he had sung 'better than Justin Timberlake'. However, it was Ellington who Will took through. 'Jaz, I want to take you on to the lives', he said. 'You have something in you. You got soul in a bowl. You got soul on a pole. You got soul you don't know! Whoa, you got soul.'

Will was relieved that things were going so well. He had harboured concerns for this round and beyond. 'I'm nervous for the first live battles,' he wrote on Twitter. 'I haven't been this nervous since we played a concert in Brazil in front of 1.5 million people.'

As the resultant live finals played out, Will admitted that he did not know why one of his acts, the much-loved Tyler James, had even entered the series. 'Tyler is an artist, a true star,' he told *Radio Times*. And I don't even know why he's in the competition because he has albums out and I'm a fan of them. He's great. And hats off to him for joining the competition when you have a career already.'

His other much fancied act was Ellington. 'Jaz is just an angel, he's a true gift,' Will said. 'He's on his way to legendary status because he has a legendary voice. We saw a star in the making in his performance.'

It was at this stage in the competition that some of the series' boasts – many of which Will was at the forefront of promoting – began to unravel. With the healthy dose of pomposity and earnestness inherent in their publicity for the show, the producers had made a rod for their own back. Having made – and emphasized so strongly – the claim that *The Voice* was different and more credible than other reality talent contests, it had positioned itself for a fall.

In the battle round, it was quickly realized by many viewers that the coaches were now in a perfect position to weed out any contestants whose appearance did not live up to their voice, thus undermining the show's unique selling point that the entire project was, as it repeatedly barked, 'all about the voice'. The *Guardian*'s influential pop-music writer Peter Robinson nailed it when he wrote: 'Behind all the bluster surely everyone involved in *The Voice* – unless pathetically deluded – knows that it's a reality show much like any other.'

The other claim, that the series would be about the contestants and not the coaches, was somewhat compromised by the row that erupted around Will's use of his smartphone during the broadcasts. After he was caught on camera using his phone during one of the live shows, Will was reportedly scolded by BBC bosses. According to the *Sunday Express*, they told him his behaviour was 'unprofessional' as well as 'rude and disrespectful'. Will, however, was unrepentant. He argued that, by using his phone to tweet, he 'wasn't being rude' but was merely conforming to the 'new way' viewers followed *The Voice*. He added a rhyming couplet to underline that he intended to continue utilizing technology as part of his involvement during the series. 'TV, phone, laptop, & tablet ... it's a new day ... if I don't tweet during live TV I'm not connecting to people watching in the new way.' All of the controversies, however, fed the publicity machine and kept the show in the public's mind.

Indeed, his tweeting was not the only thing for which Will was criticized. He travelled around the world in between the live shows, prompting accusations that he was not spending enough time coaching his acts. This was a familiar controversy of the genre. Simon Cowell had been accused of the same thing during past series of *The X Factor*.

Will defended himself in the *Mirror*. 'I've just got a different approach. My coaching is, "Hey, let's talk",' he said. He felt that his absence on other business would not harm his acts. 'I'm not worried. I don't get nervous about not being here. It all depends on how you coach. If you focus on trying to unlock the magic within you, there's no coach and no rehearsal which can bring that.'

He also insisted that his travelling was all professionally related, not an act of leisure. He had travelled so extensively, he told the *Evening Standard*, that it had made him ill. 'I'm recovering from bronchitis,' he said. 'Because I travel upon travel upon travel. If I leave here it's not like I go home and rest – I literally go to Mexico and work, and Brazil and work, Singapore and work. Since I saw you last I've probably been to eight countries.'

With his act Jaz Ellington reportedly becoming

'unpopular' backstage for behaving like a 'diva', Will was finding that *The Voice* could spark crisis headlines almost as much as the bloated, hyped *X Factor* could. In time, the show would also prompt controversy over issues as varied as Jessie J's use of the world 'lame', the perceived softness of the coaches, and Will's cutting comments about some of his rivals' acts.

The tweeting row continued re-erupting for some weeks, but Will remained defiant. 'I'm not going to stop tweeting during live shows ... I think it allows people to live the moment with me as I'm in it ... ,' he announced on the social-networking site. 'I told the bbc: "It may seem odd me tweeting ... but trust me ... this will be the norm one day & people are going to copy it".'

Then came a fresh round of headlines, this time claiming that he was 'subliminally advertising' his own fashion range on the show. Will was often featured wearing a blue-and-yellow 'superhero'-style jacket from his collection. It was unmistakably one of his creations: it even included his beloved slogan 'Go hard or go home' just beneath the left breast. In promotional photographs for the series, he is featured wearing another jacket from his range, this time a grey-and-white effort. Then, in footage of him rehearsing with his acts backstage, he was wearing an orange-and-blue jacket.

By the time the series reached its semi-final, just eight acts remained overall. Of Will's acts, Jaz Ellington impressed again with his performance of The Beatles classic 'Let It Be'. Tyler James, meanwhile, bravely took on 'Bohemain Rhapsody' by Queen. By this stage, viewers had noted Will's tendency to use the complimentary word 'dope' a lot during the shows. When Leanne Mitchell sang, Will was so impressed that he went 'dope' crazy, to the amusement of many viewers. Of Will's acts, James was the one to make it to the final, where he would compete with Bo Bruce, Mitchell and Vince Kidd. James, a former friend of Amy Winehouse, with a self-confessed colourful past of his own, was not the favourite. That honour belonged to Bruce – though there would be a twist in the tale that would send the title elsewhere.

On the night of the final, James sang Michael Jackson's 'I'll Be There' and then teamed up with his coach Will to perform Usher's 'OMG', with the pair arriving onstage in style, descending from the ceiling with the aid of harnesses. The duet was a strange one due to its bizarre choreography: Tyler seemed not entirely comfortable with the song, nor entirely at ease with the excitable presence of his coach flying and dancing around him. The climax to the song featured a masterpiece from Will, incorporating 'Vote, vote, for Tyler James' into the closing chant. Throughout the evening,

Will gave his man plenty of support and encouragement, reminding viewers how many issues he had 'overcome' and declaring him a 'superstar'. He also said he had 'learned from Tyler how to be hungry, to appreciate opportunities' and that he was 'proud to have him on my team'. Tyler described Will as not just a 'coach, but a friend'.

Will and his fellow coaches also performed a 'mash-up' of their own. The quartet performed an unlikely medley of their own songs, comprising of Will's 'Where is the Love?', Jones's 'It's Not Unusual', Jessie J's 'Price Tag', and The Script's 'Breakeven'. The final product was not half as ridiculous as one might have thought. It certainly outclassed the unintentionally comedic performance of U2's 'Beautiful Day' by the coaches earlier in the series, which had been rightly mocked on the Internet.

Will's man was not to win the series, however. James finished third, ahead of Kidd but behind the top two of Bruce and Mitchell. The final crown, for which Bruce had been so widely tipped, actually went to Mitchell. 'Oh, my God, I can't believe it,' she said. Neither could some of the final's 8.7 million viewers, though it was ultimately the voting public who had made her the victor.

The following day's press reported that Will was keen to return to the show for its second series in 2013. Announcing his intention to move to London full-time, Will said: 'I'll definitely come back.' BBC One controller Danny Cohen was said to be keen on bringing all four of the coaches back for the second series.

Will, ever the canny and speedy operator, also revealed that he had already taken three of his finalists into the studio to record. 'The annoying thing for me is people go on these shows but it takes for ever for their albums to come out,' he told the *Sunday Mirror*. 'I wanted to do *The Voice* because I want to speed up the process. I just want to come live in London and do that.'

The first significant and official release in the wake of the show put one of Will's contestants at the top of the 'chart'. A compilation featuring performances by the final eight contestants was released, and Tyler James's cover of Steve Winwood's 'Higher Love' quickly became the most downloaded track on iTunes, giving James, and his coach, a retrospective victory of sorts.

Having had concerns about what might be ahead when he first signed up to *The Voice*, Will had learned to love the show. Perhaps it was only after the series had ended that he began to grasp what an experience it had been. 'I felt very strange not doing #thevoiceuk this weekend,' he confessed on Twitter, a week after the final. 'I felt as if it was all a lovely dream and it never really happened ... #imisslondon.'

Whether the show had been a success overall became a

point of debate. A tour had been arranged in the wake of the show, in which the final eight contestants of the series were scheduled to perform at venues across Britain, including London's O2 Arena, and in other major cities, including Manchester, Birmingham, Liverpool and Cardiff. This mimicked the annual *X Factor* tour, in which the finalists follow the same route. However, in the case of *The Voice* the plan went awry when poor sales meant that the entire tour had to be called off.

Andrew Lloyd Webber criticized the series, saying that most of the finalists sang 'out of tune', while BBC Radio 2's Paul Gambaccini described the overall experience of the show as 'karaoke'. There was also embarrassment when two BBC executives, speaking at the Edinburgh Festival, failed to recall the name of the show's winner just two months after she was crowned.

A glance through the history of reality television paints a more realistic and promising picture. All of the genre's shows have had their critics and teething problems. *The X Factor*, which in terms of cold numbers remains a benchmark of success, endured a rocky opening series in which critics slammed it. The final of the first series descended into farce when Sharon Osbourne denounced its winner, Steve Brookstein, as a 'fake'. Brookstein then spectacularly fell out with all concerned before experiencing an astonishing flop.

A fact about *The Voice* that no critic can dispute is that the BBC felt sufficiently impressed with its performance to commission a second series, which will be broadcast in 2013. Putting aside the inevitable 'paper talk' surrounding which celebrities will, won't or might be coaches in series two, Will would certainly be a popular choice to return to those famous rotating chairs. While he had not won the debut series he had, more than any other person taking part, won the hearts of viewers. Will, for so long an Anglophile, was now feeling the love coming the other way more than ever.

*

In the week after he had lost Frances Wood and Joelle Moses from his team on *The Voice*, Will was thrilled to be part of the London 2012 Olympic torch procession. This satisfied a longstanding ambition on his part. In 1984, as a child, Will had sat in front of the television and watched the Olympic Games in Los Angeles. The tournament captured his imagination and made him wish he could one day have a part to play in one. His turn with the torch transported him back to 1984. 'I had that flashback when they handed me the torch to run in Taunton,' he told the *Daily Mail*. 'It's like a blast moment and a surreal moment and a can't believe it moment all at the same time.'

Will, who has appeared on primetime television, played to huge sold-out stadiums and participated in no end of other potentially nerve-wracking events, said he felt more anxious taking part in this activity than he had in anything before. The reason for his intense nerves on the day was the potential for pyrotechnic calamity. 'I got a little more nervous this time than all the things I have done,' he said. 'I am not holding a flame when I am performing in front of people and the last thing you want to do is make a mistake with fire in your hands.' He avoided such perils but managed to create a minor controversy all the same.

It all started when the torch reached Taunton in Somerset. Will was the 109th runner to take part in the seventy-day relay that covered 80,000 miles in total. It was an exciting moment for him as he set off with the torch. In keeping with his self-confessed addiction to Twitter, he tweeted about his torch-run, even as it was going on. It was with this fact, and the tweets themselves, that the controversy started. One of his tweets read: 'Thank you coca.cola for this once in a life time experience to come to taunton and #runthetorch ... Crazy energy in the uk.'

This seems innocuous enough in itself. However, while some onlookers were ambivalent about his tweeting, others were offended, feeling he was disrespecting or even desecrating the moment. To an extent, this reflected a sense of negativity about the Olympic Games that some in Britain were determined to air. It is easy, in the wake of the gloriously successful tournament, to forget how many people were convinced it would be a disaster in the weeks beforehand. Will was unfortunate just to have walked into this atmosphere of negativity.

However, his position was not helped by the fact that in some of the tweets he spelled the name of the area incorrectly. For instance, one message read: 'Its nuts here in taurton ... so much excitement ... #runningthetorch'. This unintentional spelling error only served as grist to the mill of those who were questioning why an American was even taking part in the torch procession. As he ended his part in the procession, Will felt almost euphoric. He explained why he had performed a short 'moonwalk' during a part of the run. 'I was thinking "me and Michael" ... I don't want to Tom Jones it right now,' he said afterwards. 'Me and Mike were really close and he would have been proud that I ran the torch, so I thought why not moonwalk it a couple of steps while running with the torch.'

In the days that followed, several newspapers whipped up negative headlines about Will. Judith Woods, of the *Daily Telegraph*, asked: 'Why is Will.i.Am all over us like a rash?' Complaining that Will was 'fast-tracked to National Treasure status', she entered slightly uncomfortable territory when she stated that he 'came over here on a visa for *The Voice* but, rather like the programme, overstayed his welcome'. She concluded her piece with a jokey speculation that Will might have been considering applying for the BBC Director General's job. The *Daily Mail*, as is its wont, joined in the outrage, asking: 'He's not an athlete, he's not British so why is Will.i.am carrying the Olympic flame?'

It caused much shock when he was suddenly revealed as one of the participants. One wonders how much angrier some commentators might have been had they been aware that Will had known that he was going to take part in the procession, for a year – a fact he only revealed after the run. Some writers still managed to see the lighter side of the story. A somewhat tongue-in-cheek – but still indirectly admiring – article was posted on the *Guardian*'s website. It argued: 'Will.I.Am has become a beacon of hope to us dreary Brits, with our punctuation-free names. So what a flash of genius to get him there in Taunton.'

Meanwhile, Will was too busy getting excited about the forthcoming Games themselves to lose much sleep over criticism. He declared himself a 'huge Olympics fan'. He added: 'I want to see the swimming match, I want to see Usain Bolt. I want to see if he's really that fast because I want to race him one day. I wouldn't win but I want to see how close I would come.'

Were he to take part in an Olympics, it would be track running that he would choose. 'I'm very fast,' he boasted in the *Guardian*, adding that he has been nicknamed 'Willie Zoom' due to his speed. 'I take pride in how fast I am, still to this day. I was in the studio the other day and me and Chris Brown were talking. I don't know how it came up, but I was like: "I'm fast". And he was like: "You ain't fast, man". So I said: "Let's go race!" His trainer gets in on it too, who was supposedly an ex-NFL footballer, so we're standing in the middle of the street and I asked if I could take my shoes off because I had dress shoes on – at least let me run barefoot! But they made me run in my Christian Louboutin shoes!' In his telling of the story, he was comfortably victorious in this impromptu R&B race. 'Man let me tell you they were so upset because I not only smoked them once but smoked them twice,' he boasted. 'And now people know not to mess with me. I beat Ne-Yo too! And his trainer!'

His humorous remarks certainly deflected some of the sting surrounding his interest in the Games. In the weeks after his time with the torch, other runners came in for criticism. For instance, Paloma Faith's red high heels prompted questioning headlines about how 'ridiculous' her 'unsuitable' footwear was for her stint on the torch relay. It was all part of the pre-Olympics pantomime. Will was just pleased to have taken part in the Olympic experience. His love of Britain was deepening the more embedded in and recognized by the public he became.

The ever-adoring Cheryl Cole spoke in his defence. 'I heard a couple of people say, "He's not British", but it's not about that,' she told Capital Radio. 'We're inviting people from all over the world to come and race or do whatever their part is in the Olympics in our country, everybody is welcome, so [the criticism's] not right.' She continued: 'He thoroughly enjoyed it. He carried that torch everywhere – he had it on *The Voice*. He's obsessed with it. I think he's an honorary Brit.'

An honorary Brit, indeed. As he told an interviewer for *Radio Times*, he really had fallen for Britain and the rich creative state it is currently in. 'I don't know what's brewing here, but you guys have so many great singers, from Adele to Jaz to freaking Marina and the Diamonds, to freaking Everything Everything,' he said. 'Great talent coming out of this country. Get out of here.'

Recognition of his place in the hearts of an increasingly mainstream audience came when he was invited to appear on BBC One's primetime chat show *The Graham Norton Show*. Alongside him was the actress Miriam Margolyes, and some of her remarks to Will during the broadcast took the programme to the front pages of the newspapers.

At one point, turning to Will, Margolyes said:

'Unfortunately, I don't know many black people. We don't get to meet across the colour line much except in show business and that's what's so nice.' Will, in common with much of the audience, was rather flabbergasted by what Margolyes had said. At first, he seemed unable to work out to what extent she was joking – if at all. His normally loquacious manner was nowhere to be seen.

Their fellow guest on the couch, the actor and comedian Greg Davies, tried to cut through the awkward atmosphere with the quip: 'It's exotic.' While host Norton also tried to lighten the mood, saying: 'It's lovely, Miriam, you're right.'

When Margoyles learned that Will had made a major donation to the Prince's Trust and of his other charitable works, she continued to make the atmosphere awkward. On learning he had donated nearly half a million pounds to the charity, she told Will: 'You're fabulous! How unexpected that a rapper would do this. I don't have a very positive attitude towards rappers. I don't really know any, you're the first one I've actually talked to.'

Again, for a moment, Will could hardly believe his ears, but he recovered his poise long enough to say: 'I'm the first rapper and black guy you've kicked it with!' The audience was loving the exchange and continued to do so as Will humorously taught Margolyes the meaning of the phrases: 'home boys' and 'old school'. It was a conversation that made the front pages of some of the following morning's press.

Will's new stature in Britain was symbolically reaffirmed when he was invited to play a significant part in the Queen's Diamond Jubilee celebrations. It was to be a night in which Will's role sparked considerable debate among viewers. Wearing a military-style outfit of red, white and blue, he certainly looked the part for the occasion. He was one of the first performers onstage at the London concert, performing his band's hit 'I Gotta Feeling' with his fellow *Voice* coach Jessie J. Some newspapers claimed that he had used Auto-Tune for his performance. He made a second appearance onstage to accompany soul legend Stevie Wonder in his rendition of 'Happy Birthday'. It was a strange turn for the evening to take. It was not The Queen's birthday that was being celebrated, after all. Also, as Will first reappeared on the stage in response to Wonder's beckoning, some wondered what he could add to the performance.

The answer was not much of worth. Will looked uncomfortable as he stood next to Stevie Wonder. He sang some weak backing vocals on the chorus, and added a few spontaneous ad lib comments such as 'Happy birthday, your highness', 'Put your hands up, y'all' and 'Yo'. As the song ended, and Wonder's band launched quickly into the next track, 'Superstition', Will left with no acclaim, awkwardly shuffling off the stage as the show went on without him.

Twitter, that increasingly valued barometer of public opinion, delivered a largely unimpressed verdict. One typical tweet read, 'So at what point in man's aural evolution did we resort to needing will.i.am to shout "yo" over Stevie Wonder?'

There was little comfort for Will in the knowledge that the evening's other much-criticized act was his very own client, Cheryl Cole. Her half of the duet with event organizer Gary Barlow on Lady Antebellum's 'Need You Now', left many unmoved.

It was Cole herself who, feeding the media's ongoing love of stories involving Will tweeting in inappropriate situations, claimed he had been set to Tweet while alongside the Queen onstage. 'I actually had to warn him as we walked on to the stage,' Cole told Graham Norton later. 'He had the phone at the ready. I'm not joking, I had to say to him, "Put that phone away right now before I kill you".'

Will had happily tweeted photographs of himself at the event, including one of him alongside Prince William, the prince positively towering over Will in the photograph. 'I just realized I'm the shorter "will.i.am" #diamondjubilee', Will wrote on the accompanying tweet. He also posed alongside a group of royal guardsmen, commenting that he was now 'brit.i.am'.

He also got himself snapped alongside Robbie Williams,

Sir Elton John, Sir Paul McCartney and Annie Lennox. As protocol dictated, Will was not to have a side-by-side photo of himself with the Queen, though he was officially snapped shaking her hand backstage. 'I love the queen', he Tweeted later. 'She's super dope. She reminds me of my mum. I mean, my mum and no money and the Queen is obviously loaded, but just their strength and perseverance.' His admiration for Debra is never far from Will's mind, her presence never far from his existence and work.

8 Heart and Soul

When he is interviewed by the press, Will often chooses to break off from the traditional interrogative path to read the interviewer – and therefore his or her eventual readers – text messages he has exchanged with his mother, Debra. In April 2012, he did just this when he was quizzed by *Radio Times* magazine. His rendition began with a message his mother had sent him about her involvement in his charity:

> 'Hey Willi, I want to let you know that I feel ten feet tall right now. I want to be a part of all that. I want to be involved in all these projects. I want to be part of your plan, I want to soar with you. You are the fuse that's needed to set the bombs off. It's about to explode baby boy.'

'That's cool, Mom,' Will had replied,

'That's why I put you on board. Yay.'

Debra then wrote: 'Thank you so very much. My heart feels like it will burst, I love you so very much, not for what you give me or what you've done, but for who you are. A son with a very, very big heart.'

The exchange concluded with Will writing: 'Of course, Mom. You built my heart.'

The key figure in Will's life, Debra is also now a pivotal part of one of his charities, the i.am.home Fund, which was set up to help those in jeopardy of losing their homes due to the economic crisis in America. Asked by *The New York Times* how the charity would operate, Will gave a simple description of its activity, adding that in setting it up he was ensuring he was true to the message of the campaign video he had created for Barack Obama in 2008. 'I say: "Let me pay for that house. It's yours. You don't got to pay me back." It's that simple. Why am I doing it? Because I said, "Yes We Can."'

His other foundations work in the fields of education and employment. The i.am.angel Foundation, for instance, was launched in 2009. Speaking about the charity, Will told StarCam: 'The world doesn't need another musician, they need another Bill Gates'. A man who combines those two contributions would be extraordinary – and, in the future, Will might just be that man. The opening aim of the charity was 'the idea of providing assistance to needy students wanting to attend college through a program entitled i.am. scholarship.' That scholarship program has grown and grown since. 'I know my purpose is to continue to inspire young people because it's just going to keep inspiring me back,' Will said. 'I want to do my part. I want to invest in America's future and I want to send you to college. i.am here to let you know that you can be anything you want to be. You are the future of the world.'

As well as devoting his time, energy and name to his foundations, he has also put his money where his mouth is – since 2010, he has donated a figure estimated to be in excess of £1million to them. He is passionate about his charity work and the opportunities it brings to those who sorely lack them. He told one interviewer that his primary reason for joining *The Voice* was the hope that the renewed fame it would bring him might offer him further 'leverage' in the charitable sphere. 'It's like the beginning of my philanthropic career,' he said.

He is also partnering with Coca-Cola on an interesting recycling initiative, which, with his characteristic flair for attention-grabbing word play, he has called Ekocycle (the first part of the word, 'Ekoc', is, of course, 'Coke' spelled backwards). The mission is to encourage large corporations to stop churning out waste. 'I'm like, "What if I can take their by-products and make new products?' he explained to *ES* magazine. 'What if I can take their bottles and turn them into jackets and glasses, and I could make a base cloth out of their aluminium to make bicycles and chairs and computers and phones?'

Later, he explained an even grander vision: to put Ekocycle alongside the stature of Google and Twitter in terms of vocabulary. 'The key is to "become a verb"', he said, in an interview with the *Financial Times*. 'Google became a verb. Twitter became a verb. How does Coke become a verb? Ekocycle – and you redefine the word recycle.' It is a big ambition, yet experience has shown that betting against Will achieving his dreams is a risky move.

How, many have wondered, does he manage to keep succeeding in his endeavours? Be it his music career, his business or charity, for Will, it all keeps coming back to one thing: activity. He feels that many people have lost sight of how much more valuable it is to play a good game, rather than merely talk one. In these days of online social networks, on which many people simply brag and exaggerate their achievements, lots of people have lost their way. 'People have got it all mixed up,' he said. 'Supporting is actually doing. Let's change the word "supporting" and use the word "doing". What are you doing to help America and Obama? Donating money to the campaign? Or going into communities and changing people's lives?' In a more concise encapsulation of his guiding philosophy, he said: 'If you ain't doing something you're doing nothing'.

One day, Will could publish an engrossing book of motivational wisdom. In the meantime, he stays true to his guiding philosophy and keeps on doing something. In 2012, off the back of his success on *The Voice* and his shoulder-rubbing with the British monarchy, Will teamed his charity up with The Prince's Trust. 'As a judge on *The Voice*, the people of the UK have welcomed me into their sitting rooms week after week and I feel very much at home here,' he said. 'Working with The Prince's Trust, I am joining the mission to help transform the lives of disadvantaged young people living in underprivileged neighbourhoods in the UK.'

In donating to the Trust, his thinking was that its work carries with it the potential to transform an entire neighbourhood. He used as examples the founders of Facebook and Twitter. 'If one Mark Zuckerberg comes from Brixton, then Brixton is changed forever', he told *ES* magazine. 'If one Jack Dorsey comes from East London, then East London is changed forever'.

When he met Prince Charles, the morning after the

Diamond Jubilee flotilla, it was an unlikely meeting in more than one sense. Charles, though, left Will impressed. The Prince had just found out that his father, the Duke of Edinburgh, had been hospitalized with a bladder infection. 'So it was heavy,' Will said. 'He spoke very passionately about inner cities and philanthropy, and I got into the car afterwards and I thought: "That guy is something else" – because he had just found out about his father but he still kept the meeting. That guy is awesome.'

With the aforementioned i.am.home arm of the charity, we can return to the start of Will's story. All too often, people who have achieved vast riches through their fame make the proud boast that they have never forgotten where they came from. Sometimes, these claims are little more than vanity – a declaration of self-interested lip service to the communities they left behind. In Will's case, the sentiment is far more sincere. 'The reason I started i.am. home is because I come from poverty,' he said. 'I survived and came out of it because you guys support my music. My one day dream was to have a house, buy a house for my mom and take care of family.'

As we have seen, he fulfilled that dream, and enjoyed one of the proudest moments of his life as he did so. For the never-satisfied, ever active Will, that proud moment only awakened in him a desire to do more of the same.

'Now that I've achieved that goal I can't forget what it was like – living on the verge. Helping out families in need is a personal venture. Something I feel I need to do.' The word 'need' underlines so much of his existence: it is a need, more than a desire, that drives so much of Will's ferocious, frenetic lifestyle. His engine is oft powered involuntarily.

The rewards of his resultant stature keep on coming. Not all are rewards of richness or fame, some are just the places his status can take him to, the experiences it brings to him. In the spring of 2012, he revealed that NASA had approached him to write the first song to played on the planet Mars. 'I don't think I can talk about it, but there is a rocket going to Mars,' he told Graham Norton on his show. 'It lands in August and when in lands it will send back a signal to earth and that signal will be the song.'

This project with NASA is to help inspire kids to get involved in science, technology, engineering and mathematics. 'My mission is to inspire the youth to care about education.' This out-of-this-world project would take Will's quest to inspire to a whole new dimension. He could hardly wait for it to happen.

As for his activity on planet Earth, Will remains as restless as ever. In July 2012, he passed another milestone when he enjoyed his first UK number one as a solo artist. Thanks in part to his successful appearance on *The Voice*, and the accompanying stature it gave him in the UK, his single 'This is Love' hit the top of the British singles chart. For Will, this was a moment of substantial pride. He felt he had proved some of his doubters wrong. 'I've had number ones before with The Black Eyed Peas, but to me this one means so much, because I know people thought I can only be successful in The Black Eyed Peas. They were wrong,' he said.

He had collaborated with Eva Simons on the track, and spoke with enormous passion about her talent. 'There are a lot of girls that are pretty and that can sing a little bit,' he said. 'And they are usually connected to some powerful dude that gets them a whole bunch of songs that some unknown people did in the bedroom.' Somewhat uncomfortably, many might feel this description would apply to Cheryl Cole. It is unlikely Will would agree with that, but there is no doubting how much Simons had energized him. 'So whenever I switch gears musically or change directions, it's because of the adrenaline and the influence of being around the world and dealing with different people like Eva,' he said.

He continued work on his next solo album, *#willpower*, which he hoped to fashion into a complex work, replete with a number of different styles. 'There's classical s**t, like just me and a guitar and an orchestra or me with just an orchestra and a kid's choir,' he said. 'There's some ghetto, ugly, dirty stuff. And then there's dance stuff, global world stuff and, like, avant garde, left-of-centre, for-art's-sake music that has nothing to do with getting played on the radio. I'm just art-ing out. It's pretty diverse.'

Originally, the album's title had been *Black Einstein*. Fergie had first announced the original name on Hollyscoop.com. 'I believe Will is coming out with a solo album, I've heard it, it's called *Black Einstein*, and it's amazing,' she said. 'I've been waiting for him to come out with this for so long, 'cause I want it. He won't give it to me. I want it for the gym. He's so amazing. Such a genius lyricist and I'm really excited for his project.'

Work on the album took place predominantly in Los Angeles, London and Paris. Will was deliberately taking his time on it. 'I didn't want to force this album,' he told *Boombox*. His fear that self-indulgence might lead to him losing his grasp on reality was clear. 'A lot of times an artist can over-think things. You get to the point that you are so wrapped up in your music that you feel like you can just put buffalo knuckle sound effects on a track. It's like, "Yo, you seriously making buffalo knuckle noises on a beat and you think that's hot?"' Instead, he hooked-up with some of the cream of the music scene: 'I worked with LMFAO. I got songs with Chris Brown, Ne-Yo, Britney Spears and a few other people,' he said.

Whether on his solo material or on other artists' own albums, Will is often to be found in the recording studio. In September 2012, he worked in the studio with former Pussycat Doll Nicole Scherzinger. She tweeted a photograph of them at work, with the message: 'Me and @iamwill in the studio … making la la la la la's in LA.' Will loved it. 'I made this song with Nicole Scherzinger that you would never expect,' he said. 'This classic piece of music that I did with Nicole, it's beautiful. That girl sings like I've never heard anybody sing like that in pop culture.'

One day as they worked, an earthquake shook Los Angeles. Will quipped on Twitter: 'There was a #Earthquake in l.a just 1min ago ... If it wasn't ... it was the beat I'm making in the studio for @NicoleScherzy... #califault. [sic].'

He has also recently worked with Rita Ora, who offered an interesting insight into his style of work after he produced her song 'Fall in Love'. 'will.i.am is incredible,' she told *Digital Spy*. 'He's like a genius and he works so fast. I don't know how his brain is so like ... He can do so many things at once and does it the best as well. He doesn't half-heartedly do anything. We did "Fall in Love" in a day and night and then we went out and had a drink.'

He has also worked with the young prince of pop himself, Justin Bieber. Will has described the Canadian sensation as his 'little brother'. 'I like him because he's going to be around for a long time,' he told MTV News. 'And he's really talented ... [He is] very talented, beyond what people probably think he's capable of. I've worked with him and [seen] how talented he is.' There were certainly no 'cool' points to be had in making this sort of statement, but Will preferred to tell it as he saw it. He continued: 'In the industry, especially as it's changing, you're going to [need] some type of real talent. Maybe people can't see [it], right now, but ten, fifteen years from now, he'll still be around.'

Speaking of longevity, another of the artists Will worked with on *#willpower* is one of the record industry's longest-lasting icons: Mick Jagger. The Rolling Stones frontman appears on one of the album's singles, 'T.H.E. (The Hardest Ever)'. Will was pleasantly surprised by the ease with which he secured Jagger's involvement, particularly following the rather starry, distant way the Stones had behaved when the Black Eyed Peas toured with them. Rather than having to embark on a lengthy, quid pro quo negotiation via gate-keepers, due to a relationship he had built with Jagger since The Black Eyed Peas opened for the Rolling Stones in 2007, Will was simply able to call Jagger directly to ask him if he was interested in guest-appearing on the song.

The two had struck up an immediate rapport back-stage. 'Mick and I got along really well,' he told the *Mirror*. 'He took my number and wherever he was in the world he would text me to hang out. "Yo, Will, I'm in Brazil. Are you here?" or "I'm in LA, where are you at?" Eventually, we hung out in 2008 at a technology conference in New York. You wouldn't believe we have similar friends that are tech enthusiasts. We have so much in common. And of course he showed me his famous strut at the bar.'

So, when Will contacted Jagger afresh to enquire about a collaboration, he got an affirmative response. 'Come down,' Jagger told him, 'I want to hear the song.' Once the old rocker heard it, he agreed to join Will in the studio the very next day to record his part. Will's long-term producer and friend Jimmy Iovine could hardly believe his luck when he got the chance to produce a song featuring Jagger. He put the scale of his excitement into words for Will when he said, 'When I was younger I wanted to be Mick Jagger – what A Tribe Called Quest is to you, that was Mick for me.'

Will believes in striking while the iron is hot, and life has sometimes cruelly shown this to be a sensible approach. The year 2012 began with the unexpected death of another icon with whom Will had worked. Whitney Houston died in Los Angeles at the age of forty-eight. When Will heard of her death, he posted his immediate feelings on Twitter. 'I'm so sad, Whitney Houston was so kind, sweet, wonderful, amazing, talented and a true gift to the world', he tweeted. He added later: '#iwillalwaysloveyou'.

Later still, when Will remembered working with the soul star, his memories included the omnipresent figure of his mother, Debra. 'When I was working with Whitney Houston she reminded me of my mom, just how graceful and polite she was,' he told the *Guardian*. 'I told Whitney this and she said: "Let me see the proof of that, you should bring her down!" I called up and said: "Ma, get your butt down to my house this minute! Whitney Houston wants to see you so she can see your personality!" She loved Whitney.'

It was a testing start to what was proving a typically industrious year for Will.

Meanwhile, there were other challenges to be negotiated. He and his two male bandmates filed a lawsuit against their former financial adviser, Sean Larkin, accusing him of costing them over $3 million (£1.8 million). (Fergie has her own separate financial manager and therefore was uninvolved in this suit.) Their suit claimed that Sean M. Larkin 'falsely represented ... on numerous occasions that he was taking care of everything and that they had nothing to worry about', according to a report in the *Los Angeles Times*. Larkin had, several months previously, admitted in a deposition that he had 'got in over my head with the amount of clients I had'.

Will had another problem when his car was stolen as

he attended the launch party for his own solo album. He had been photographed alongside the car as he arrived at the bash at the Avalon Hotel in Beverly Hills, but when he left at 2 a.m. it was nowhere to be seen. 'My car was stolen ... what the f**k,' he wrote on Twitter. 'Where is my f**king car ...??? This isn't funny anymore. I'm going to be optimistic and pray that my car is returned and safe. #givemebackmycar this joke is getting old ...'

His use of the word 'joke' to describe what had happened was precise: Will believed that there was a good chance the car's disappearance was more of a prank than a crime. For that reason, he stated on Twitter, he did not intend immediately to contact the police about the disappearance of his custom-made DeLorean. 'I'm not going to the police ... spread the word via tweets in case I'm getting punk'd', he wrote. 'I don't want to waste tax dollars on pranks #wheresmycar'.

He later returned to Twitter, to write: 'I'm going to be optimistic and pray that my car is returned and is safe', adding that he believed the punishment for its disappearance should be 'hard and swift'. Two months earlier the car had been impounded by police after it was found to be unregistered.

Prior to the car disappearance, the biggest story at Will's party had been the arrival of a scantily clad Lindsay Lohan.

The controversial, much-derided socialite announced that she wanted to work with Will. How he took that news is unknown. However, he was thrilled when he discovered his car had been found by businessman Ryan Friedlinghaus. Will tweeted: 'my car has been found ... #bestnewsever thank you so much ryan ...' However, on the car being returned to him, Will quickly discovered that some of its contents were missing. He hired private detectives to probe the mystery.

*

His enigmatic personal life continued to draw much speculation. In April, he was rumoured to be dating the former Spice Girl, Geri Halliwell. When she joined him at the Rose Club in London, where he was performing a short solo set, tongues were set wagging. 'It definitely seemed like they were on a date,' the ubiquitous, unnamed 'eye-witness' told the *Sun*. 'They were both really giggly with each other and were laughing all night. They arrived separately and left again at different times.' Within weeks, Halliwell was revealed to be dating not Will but another celebrity – kooky comedian Russell Brand.

At the time of writing, Will's preferences remain mysterious. On the rare occasions that he speaks about his sex life, he tends to masterfully balance each revelation with a further smoke-screen, forever leaving the world guessing. 'I'm not a gold digger, I'm a boob digger,' he told the *Sun* in 2010. 'I like boobs. But I was always the homie, the friend, rather than the lover. I'd have a crush on a girl and she'd say, "I don't know, Will, I see you as my brother".'

In a rare candid moment, he told *ES* magazine what romance was like for him. He said that, for him, it is 'just deep'. He added: 'Then I like… [huge pause] then I get deep. Like, almost spiritual. Like spiritual and science. The marriage of the two. For me, love is like … that's why it's hard. I like talking about deep shit. Just lying in bed, snuggle-wuggles, conversation. I like to communicate, conversate, dive into freakin' theories.'

He entered more comfortable territory when, in early August 2012, he drove to NASA mission control to watch the Curiosity Rover land on Mars. At the Jet Propulsion Laboratory (JPL) in Pasadena, California, he watched with childlike wonderment as the rover touched down in the early hours of the morning. He was there to listen as his song, 'Reach for the Stars', was the first piece of music ever to be broadcast back to Earth from Mars. He shared his excitement with his Twitter following. 'I'm here @ #jpl ... I am proud to care and have passion for #stem ... watching humanity at its finest ...' he wrote. The song was beamed

300 million miles back to Earth, so it could be heard at the JPL, where NASA staff danced and cheered as the accomplishment was confirmed.

NASA Administrator Charles Bolden said: 'will.i.am has provided the first song on our playlist of Mars exploration.'

'It seems surreal,' said Will. Wearing a grey suit as he spoke to a student audience, he added: 'I didn't want to do a song that was done on a computer. I wanted to show human collaboration and have an orchestra there and something that would be timeless, and translated in different cultures, not have like a hip-hop beat or a dance beat. A lot of times ... people in my field aren't supposed to try to execute something classical, or orchestral, so I wanted to break that stigma.'

This attention to detail was extraordinary. Even when he was breaking the boundary of having the first song played from Mars, Will was ensuring that he broke musical boundaries while doing so. Including in the recording a forty-piece orchestra, complete with French horns, he had handed the song a cinematic, iconic flavour. There was widespread respect for Will in the wake of his achievement. Only the *Register* and MSN, it seemed, had an issue with the broadcast, the former describing it as: 'A depressing day for space and technology', while MSN mocked the song's lyrics, and sneered: 'We can't help thinking there are better songs to have introduced music to the Red Planet with'.

Just hours after he had celebrated his Mars moment, Will was brought crashing back to earth when he crashed his Cadillac into a parked car in Los Angeles. One way or another, the summer of 2012 was not proving to be a happy one in automotive terms. Following what he described as 'a long day and night' in the recording studio with Cheryl Cole, at 3.30 a.m., with Cheryl in the passenger seat beside him, Will accidentally smashed his £100,000 car into a parked vehicle. Eyewitnesses said that his airbag opened and struck him in the face. Though the contact gave him a nosebleed, it certainly saved him from a potentially worse fate.

Cole's passenger airbag failed to work, and she was reportedly thrown face first into the car's plush dashboard. She, too, was left with a nosebleed and bruising. Photographs of her clutching her face, with blood pouring from her nose were quickly snapped by fast-moving photographers. Police were called to the scene and the pair went to Cedars Sinai hospital. Will emerged later wearing a neck brace.

As is his custom, Will used Twitter to speak to the world about the incident. 'Car accidents are not dope,' he tweeted. 'I'm glad I'm OK'. In a follow-up tweet, he wrote: 'We're fine. Cheryl Cole [and I] were coming back from the studio but she and I are fine ... just a little wiplash [sic]'.

Will's manager, Polo Molina, then also logged on to Twitter: 'Just spoke to @iamwill, everything is OK. He and Cheryl Cole are both fine. It was a minor fender bender after a long day/night in the studio'.

Cole completed the online reassurance-fest, writing: 'Don't worry me and @iamwill are fine, promise'. Cole quickly made light of the incident, telling Capital Breakfast co-presenter Lisa Snowdon that it was Will's loquaciousness that was to blame for what occurred. 'He's a bad talker. He was talking the face off us,' she said. 'He was talking about NASA and Mars and his song.' Cole, who had to wear a black sling around her arm, also jokingly dubbed herself a 'one-arm bandit' on Twitter.

Looking ahead to 2013, as well as more cinematic dabbling – having also voiced a character in the animated 2011 film *Rio* – Will planned to learn more about technology, by signing up for a computer programming course. 'Next year I am going to school to take a computer science course,' he told the *Mirror*. 'When I am fifty-seven I still want to be relevant in popular culture and the way to be relevant within popular culture in the future is writing code. Code writers, they are my idols. Songwriters are cool – I can write songs, too – and bloggers are cool, but code writers? Those are the coolest in the world. When I was seventeen I had a dream and all the dreams I have had since seventeen I have done them beyond what I thought I was ever going to do. So now I want to go back to school and learn how to write code so I can participate in this whole new era that we are in. Writing songs is dope but writing code is better.'

Just twelve years earlier, Will had almost torn his hair out with frustration when The Black Eyed Peas album *Bridging the Gap* was leaked on Napster. Then, the world of technology seemed a dark, mysterious villain for a while. Now, he saw the virtual world just the same way he saw the 'real' world: as a playground, alive with opportunities for creativity, fun and profit.

The man who was so caught out by the emergence of Napster, has become one of the industry's most sharpest observers of the drastic changes that emerging technology is causing for the industry. He has even been appointed 'director of creative innovation' at technology giant Intel.

'There are no more dreamers,' Will told the *Financial Times*. 'I am dreaming for Intel, to rethink what a computer is going to be.' Since those dark days when he felt powerless as The Black Eyed Peas tracks were leaked ahead of release, he has grasped the nettle of technology and is now as in control of its seemingly relentless forces as it is possible to be. 'Technology is so big right now,' he told *Boombox*. 'It's that advanced, man. You can set your own studio up with a microphone that you bought from Best Buy. You can record your vocals on to your laptop and put a little compression on it because everybody is listening to music now on their phones and computers. Nobody listens to music on big systems anymore like back in the *Thriller* days.'

The latter trend is key: with large, bass-heavy speakers now becoming a thing of the past in many homes, musicians have to create music that works on the sometimes weak and tinny speakers of smartphones, pods, pads and computers. Yet for dance acts, the music also has to sound good on the huge speakers of nightclubs. Furthermore, as soon as the industry gets its collective head around one development, along comes another to change the rules once again. It is an industry in astonishing flux. Will is one of the figures who have some sense of what is happening; do not bet against him.

Although he has ruled himself out of a future in politics – he has said he believes he would quickly be assassinated were he to become a proper politician – Will seems likely to step back into that sphere at some stage. In the Spring of 2012, he was approached by David Axelrod, communications director for President Obama's re-election campaign, to see if he could conjure up a sequel to the 2008 'Yes We Can' video to help Obama's campaign. Although Will tried, he was unable to come up with a concept that he felt was worthy of consideration on the same scale as his viral 2008 video.

He eschewed an immediate encore more out of a sense of high standards than an overall unwillingness. 'Obama has done a great deal as President up to this point and I don't care about any backlash,' he told the *Sun*. 'I don't follow waves or trends or emotions. If I did I would never have supported Obama in the first place. Being President is not a two-year fix. It's got to be an eight-year ride and I'm in there with him. It took us eight years under Bush to get us in this mess. At least give the dude eight years to get us out of it. Give the guy a chance. I saw him at The White House a few months ago and he was finding it tough. We need to get behind him as a country.'

He said that Obama's 2012 election opponent Mitt Romney was making a key mistake in the 2012 election battle by allowing his supporters to push the wrong button. 'People say Romney ran businesses and that means he should be president,' he told the *Financial Times*. 'America isn't a business. America needs to be like a parent – what's good for our kids, where are they going to school, how can you guide them? Imagine if your parent was Enron and raised you like that,' he laughed. 'You don't want that dad.'

*

It is his restlessness that continues to define Will. He has offered up a possible answer as to why he cannot seem to sit still: he suffers from tinnitus. This condition leaves sufferers with a regular 'ringing' sound in one or both of their ears. There is no external source for the sound, which sometimes varies from a ringing one to one better described as a buzzing, roaring, hissing or even whistling. Sometimes sufferers experience the sound more or less constantly, others experience only sporadic episodes.

Will has suffered badly from it, to the extent that he said: 'I don't know what silence sounds like any more. Music is the only thing which eases my pain.' This, he concludes, is one of the biggest drivers of his phenomenal work rate. 'I can't be still. Work calms me down. I can't be quiet as that's when I notice the ringing in my ears. There's always a beep there every day, all day. Like now. I don't know exactly how long I've had this but it's gradually got worse.'

Even during interviews with the press, journalists have noticed how Will sometimes presses a finger into one of his ears. His statement that work calms him down is revelatory. This reversal of the more usual human experience – that it is leisure, not work, that is relaxing – explains to a large extent why he so enjoys professional activity. It should not, as we have seen throughout these pages, be taken as a definitive explanation, though.

Will's ambition and his sharp focus on the commercial potential of life is not universally admired. Some music-industry figures of generations past have wondered what happened to putting artistry ahead of commerce. The spectre of the tortured artist, willing to disappear from the public eye for years at a time, rather than working and promoting relentlessly, is now a rare one. The twenty-first-century celebrity is often a stranger to idleness, unlike many of their twentieth-century equivalents.

Of this generation's headline acts, perhaps only Adele operates in the old-fashioned style. Almost all the other big names seem to work at a more frantic rate. This is beginning to draw criticism from the old guard, who feel that today's stars have their priorities wrong. Damon Albarn of Blur has taken personal aim at Will to this end. 'I mean, will.i.am was a miserable old sod,' he told XFM radio. 'Wearing his own stuff – what is that all about? Never wearing anything other than this quasi-*Star Trek*, slightly rubbery bondage kind of stuff. Is there never a day when he wears an old T-shirt?'

Will is, as he likes to put it himself, too busy turning his own dreams into reality to let the criticism trouble him. He never gets used to the trappings of his fame, and the boyish side of him never wants to. More often than not, his every task excites him, however many times he has done it before. His nerves might never entirely lift. 'It's like I've never been on stage before,' he told the *Daily Star*. 'I've played to a million people in Brazil at the World Cup and at the Super Bowl. You'd think I have nerves of steel, but I feel brand-new again.'

He has also admitted: 'It's amazing all the love I'm getting. I was talking to apl ... and saying it feels like 2002 again for me. 2002 was when "Where is the Love?" was about to kick off. In 2012, it's a different level.'

As well as performing and producing, he will also continue to manage and mentor other artists, including Cheryl Cole. He claims to have a long-term plan in place for her. 'The Cheryl that we know now is different from the one we're going to know ten years from now,' he has vowed. Should his words come true, this could make for a fascinating turn of events.

The wheels of Will's breathless, creative and ambition-driven life continue to turn. Where will they take him next? The sense of urgency that has driven him for so long continues unabated. 'I'm too, like, right now right now right now right now right now,' he said of how he operates. 'Impatient is not the right word. It's angst. Let's go. Right now.'

We return to his hard-knock childhood growing up in the ghetto: an experience that continues to inform and motivate him, but something he is at pains to never glamorize. 'I come from the projects, but I chose to go this route,' he said of his career. 'I don't wanna remember the s*** I saw, I don't wanna talk about my friends that got shot: I wanna do music that makes me happy. Dark music gives me anxiety. I get scared! That's why Black Eyed Peas' s*** is happy, because I can get inside it and feel comfortable. I can escape from the world and go and live in the music.' The man who is will.i.am in 2012 is scarcely different from the boy who was Will growing up in the 1970s and 80s: both love to dream and to escape.

Away from work, what could Will's personal life look like in the future? Might he finally take his foot off the gas of his many professional endeavours and let a truly special someone into his life one day? 'Working hard and looking to the future is what will.i.am is all about,' said Will, the third-person vernacular he chose to hide behind proving unable to mask the sincerity of his statement. Even when he admits to personal ambitions, there is a grander mission underpinning them. 'Soon I want to settle down and have lots of girl babies, because I don't want to add to the destruction of the planet,' he told the *Guardian* in 2008. 'It's a man's world, and I think it's gonna be a female that changes it all.'

It is not hard to understand which female in Will's life gave him such a quasi-feminist perspective on the human race.

Bibliography

Sweet Revenge: The Intimate Life of Simon Cowell,
Tom Bower, Faber & Faber, 2012

Fallin' Up: My Story, Taboo of the Black Eyed Peas with
Steve Dennis, Touchstone 2011

Index

Index

Index

Index

Index